To Sarah
Without whom nothing

STEPHEN TOMKINS has a PhD in
Church History from London Bible
College. He is a freelance writer
and a regular contributor to the
Ship of Fools website and Christian
History Institute in the USA.

JOHN WESLEY
A BIOGRAPHY

STEPHEN TOMKINS

William B. Eerdmans Publishing Company
Grand Rapids, Michigan / Cambridge U.K.

The author asserts the moral right
to be identified as the author of this work

First published 2003 in the U.K. by
Lion Publishing plc
Mayfield House, 256 Banbury Road,
Oxford OX2 7DH, England

This edition published 2003
in the United States of America by
Wm. B. Eerdmans Publishing Co.
255 Jefferson Ave. S.E., Grand Rapids, Michigan 49503 /
P.O. Box 163 Cambridge CB3 9PU U.K.
www.eerdmans.com

Printed in the United States of America

07 06 05 04 03   7 6 5 4 3 2 1

ISBN 0-8028-2499-4

ACKNOWLEDGMENTS
My thanks to Dr Williams' Library, the John Rylands
University Library of Manchester, the Wesley Centre for
Applied Theology, the Christian Classics Ethereal Library
and the Wesley's Chapel Leysian Centre.

Contents

CHAPTER 1

A TROUBLED PREHISTORY

'All your Conflicts past'
From 'Soldiers of Christ, arise'

The rectory in the Lincolnshire village of Epworth was a timber building with a thatched roof – charming, comfortable and easy to burn down. On Thursday night, 9 February 1709, it burned to the ground. It was not an accident, according to the rector, Samuel Wesley – it was an attack from some of his more disgruntled parishioners, and it was not the first.

Samuel's daughter Hetty was woken by sparks falling on her feet from the thatch. While she ran to wake her mother, the rector, asleep downstairs, was roused by shouts of 'Fire!' from the road. He ran through the smoke to wake the other seven children and the servants. The maid grabbed the babies and herded the older ones, but as they converged in the hall they found themselves surrounded by flames, the front door ablaze and the roof on the point of collapse. Samuel and the maid managed to get the children downstairs and out through the back door and windows, but Mrs Wesley was too ill and heavily pregnant for such antics, so, after several attempts, she said a prayer and walked naked out through the front door.

As they gathered in the garden with the neighbours, someone heard a cry from upstairs. One of the children was missing. The five-year-old John was still in the attic where no one had woken him. Repeatedly, Samuel tried to get up the burning stairs, but they would not take his weight. In the end, he gathered the family and they knelt in prayer to commend John's soul to the Lord. Fortunately, a crowd of onlookers had also gathered, because while the Wesleys were praying a face appeared at the attic window.

John had woken in his curtained bed, and, finding the room light, he assumed it was morning and called the maid to get him up. When no one came, he stuck his head out and found the ceiling on fire. He tried the door, only to find the landing floor alight. And so he climbed on the chest by the window and leaned across. There was no time to fetch a ladder, but one man standing on the shoulders of another managed to reach him. Just as they pulled him out, the roof collapsed inwards. There was never a hope that any of their things could be saved, but Samuel called his neighbours to come and kneel with him in prayer again to give thanks. 'He has given me all my eight children: let the house go, I am rich enough.'

This early experience of salvation had a lasting impact on John Wesley's life, quite apart from allowing it to continue. We have in it all the elements for a parable of the gospel that he was to preach: the impending fiery fate, the futility of his own efforts to escape it and the unexpected heroic rescue, which he was free – but not such a fool – to decline and to which he could contribute nothing more than putting his trust in it. The incident became a favourite children's story after his death and pictures of it sat beside Moses in the bulrushes and the flight of the Holy Family to Egypt in working-class homes. Wesley came to see himself, in a favourite biblical phrase that he inscribed on one of his portraits, as 'a brand plucked from the burning', a life both generously spared and saved from hell. His mother Susanna helped to implant this idea, as so much else, in his mind. As she wrote in her spiritual notebook, 'I do intend to be more particularly careful of the soul of this child, that Thou hast so mercifully provided for, than ever I have been.' She was as good as her word.

Surveying the blackened wreckage in the morning, the rector found two scraps of paper from his treasured library, blown out of the fire into the garden, as if the visiting fiery Providence had deigned to leave him a note. They were the remnants of the two pursuits that got him through life – writing and study. The first was one of his own hymns – 'Behold the saviour of mankind', later to be a powerful favourite in his sons' mission. The other was a charred fragment of his polyglot Bible, reading, *'Vade, vende omnia quae habes et attolle crucem, et sequerere me!'* – 'Give up all that you have and take up the cross and follow me!'

What kind of pastor was this who inspired arson and attempted murder from his flock? Equally, as the only evidence we have that it was not an accident is the word of the sleeping rector, we might ask what kind of pastor would automatically assume that the fire was a congregational attempt on his life.

A quick flick through the previous few generations might not only help introduce the family John was born into, but acclimatize us a little to an England that is very distant and foreign to those of us who live in it today. The country had just emerged from a period of great religious and political turmoil: a civil war between an Anglo-Catholic king and a Puritan parliament, and a 20-year Puritan revolution. Susanna's and Samuel's ancestors were on the Puritan side; Susanna's great grandfather, for example, had helped to bring about King Charles's first minister's execution by the revolutionary parliament, while her grandfather chaired its commission into clerical abuses, publishing a controversial bestseller *The Century of Scandalous Priests*. After parliament killed the king too, his son Prince Charles led a failed uprising. It was Bartholomew Wesley, Samuel's grandfather, who stopped Charles fleeing the country at Lyme Regis. The Puritan regime abolished the monarchy, episcopacy and the House of Lords, along with a host of lesser evils, such as Christmas and the theatre, and introduced the unprecedented policy of religious toleration. Meanwhile Samuel's other grandfather, John White, was one of the architects of another Puritan experiment – the settlement at Massachusetts.

Both Samuel's and Susanna's fathers were Puritan ministers in Cromwell's radically reformed Church of England, but in 1660, Charles II was restored to the throne. In an overwhelming conservative backlash, Puritan ministers were expelled en masse in 1662, including these two fathers. The same year, Samuel was born. The Dissenting churches suffered brutal repression and although Samuel's father died eight years later, Susanna's became the most influential leader of the London Dissenters.

Clearly, Samuel and Susanna were from redoubtable Puritan stock, but they both rebelled against their rebellious upbringing. Samuel was a gifted orphan and, as Dissenters were barred from university, friends clubbed together to send him to the Dissenting Academy in London at the age of 15. In 1683, he was set an assignment to refute an Anglican tract against the Dissenters. He read the tract, was convinced by it and, without a word to anyone, set out before dawn on foot for Oxford and the establishment. It was not a merely intellectual conversion, if there is such a thing. He was disillusioned with Dissenting subculture and had profoundly royalist instincts. Once at Oxford (where he would have an inferior education to that provided by the academy, but infinitely better prospects), he paid his university expenses by waiting on rich students and doing their homework, teaching and, at first, with funds that had never been repaid to his Dissenting sponsors. Around the same time, Susanna converted – a far more cerebral conversion than Samuel's, even though she was only 13.

By this time, parliament had split for the first time into two parties, over the question of whether or not to let the Catholic James II succeed to the throne when Charles II died. The Whigs, letting their religion overcome their royalism, opposed his succession; the Tories, letting their royalism overcome their religion, supported it. Samuel and Susanna, reacting against their upbringing were to be lifelong Tories.

The year 1688 saw 'The Glorious Revolution'. As the name suggests, it proved more popular than its Puritan predecessor, uniting Anglicans with Dissenters and Tories with Whigs. When it turned out that James II planned to restore England to Catholicism, they got rid of him and replaced him with the Protestants William III and Mary. That same month, Samuel and Susanna married. As the Wesleys settled down to producing their large family, England settled down to an age of political stability and religious reaction.

In 1695, the Wesleys moved to Epworth, where the living was a reward from Queen Mary for Samuel's loyalty. He was also getting a little popularity from his recently published long poem *The Life of Christ*. An earlier book of poems called *Maggots* had not gone down so well.[*]

The real brooding presence over the Wesley household was

---

[*] 'Maggot', in the 17th century, could mean 'a piece of whimsy', but the pun is intended. The poems include not only 'On a Maggot', but such tasteful odes as 'On A Supper of Stinking Ducks' and 'The Bear Fac'd Lady'. The poetry is gloriously, monumentally awful. *The Life of Christ* earned the distinction of a place in Pope's Temple of Dullness in *The Dunciad*, but dullness is not a failing of *Maggots*.

Susanna. Married at 19, with an intellect to rival her husband's and far greater management skills, Susanna had no choice but to devote her life to rearing, educating and regimenting children. She gave birth to somewhere between 17 and 19 children, nine of whom lived to adulthood. She herself was probably the 25th child of her father, by his second wife. The figures are approximate, as in later years both fathers were rather hazy about how many children they had had.

In *The Life of Christ*, Samuel extolled her as the ideal submissive Christian wife:

Yet still I bore an undisputed sway,
   Nor was't her task, but pleasure, to obey;
Scarce thought, much less could act, what I denied,
   In our low house their was no room for pride;
Nor need I e'er direct what still was right,
   She studied my convenience and delight.
Nor did I for her care ungrateful prove,
   But only used my power to show my love.

No room for pride, indeed. If this sounds like the delusion of a man who is not equipped to deal with his wife's humanity, then the events of 1701–1702 bear up that impression.

The majority of English people had welcomed the accession of William III 13 years previously, or had soon grown to, although a strong fringe of dissent continued for years. Even many staunch Tories such as the Wesleys embraced him – or at least, Samuel assumed the Wesleys did; he evidently saw no reason to discuss the matter with his wife. Then one day, as they were gathered with their six children and the servants for morning prayers, he noticed something was wrong. When they had finished their devotions, he summoned Susanna to his study.

'Sukey,' he demanded, 'why did you not say "Amen" this morning to the prayer for the king?'

Susanna was taken aback, but explained that, as James II was unlawfully overthrown, she did not believe William of Orange to be king.

'If that be the case,' answered the rector, 'you and I must part; for if we have two kings, we must have two beds.'

That, at least, is the story as it was later passed on via John. Samuel's actual tack, according to Susanna's letters at the time, was rather more histrionic: falling to his knees, he called down the wrath of God on himself and all his posterity if he ever touched her or came to her bed, until she begged God's pardon and his for her sin. Susanna, if not as hot-headed, was equally stubborn (a characteristic John would inherit in full measure). She argued that his oath was itself unlawful, his conjugal obligation to her being as great as hers to him. 'Since I'm willing to let him quietly enjoy his opinions, he ought not to deprive me of my little liberty of conscience.' She would submit to William III as the law and Christian duty demanded, but to pray for a usurper would be to share in his sins, she felt.

So Samuel separated from her and went to London, where he happened to be going anyway to serve as proctor to Convocation. In March 1702, the offending king died. Both the Wesleys accepted his successor, Anne, but Samuel would have no reconciliation without repentance. In fact, he was looking for a naval chaplaincy, as he had had most lucratively before marrying. Susanna lived in shame and fear for her six children's future, but wrote that such feelings were nothing compared with keeping a clear conscience: 'and how I can do that if I mock almighty God, by begging pardon for what I think no sin, is past my discerning'. However, she added, 'I'm more easy in the thought of parting, because I think we are not likely to live happily together.'

Late that summer, Samuel came home for two days to tie up some loose ends and then left for good. On the road, a passing pastor told him to go back and try again. Samuel went home and prevaricated. While he was in two minds, Providence visited him with fire, as, it seems, was its wont. This time, the house was only half burned down – 'fired by one of my servants', concluded the charitable rector. This, of course, was not the same fire as we met at the start of the chapter, as that was six years later. This one, though, was to have just as much of an impact on our story in its own way for the rector was now fully persuaded to stay, take care of his family and be reconciled to his wife. Less than a year later, on 28 June 1703, John Wesley was born.

CHAPTER 2

THE RECTOR'S WIFE
(1703–13)

'The Arms of Love that compass me'
From 'Jesus! The name high over all'

The family that John grew up in was overwhelmingly female. The eldest child, Samuel, was also a boy, but as he was 12 years old when John was born, he was sent off to school in Westminster the following year. This left John with his five elder sisters – Emily, Susanna, Mary, Hetty (short for Mehetabel) and Anne – and the maid. Their rather distant father taught them ancient languages; their mother taught them everything else.

Their parents went on to have one more surviving boy and two girls: Martha, Charles and Kezia (Kezia being the child with whom Susanna was pregnant when we first met her in the fire). As she forbade her children to play with any others of the parish or to talk with the servants, it is safe to say that John's childhood was lacking in male influence – a fact that is reflected in his curious relationships with women in later life.

Nevertheless, if we were to visit Epworth rectory in these years, what would stand out, I imagine, more than the femininity of the environment is, considering the number of children it contained, its quietness. Susanna did us the favour of leaving a detailed record of her child-rearing principles, in answer to a request by John, and she allowed 'no such thing as loud talking or playing'. The idea of children being seen and not heard was not a Victorian invention, and, as she now recalled, she introduced hers to it at an early age:

When turned a year old (and some before), they were taught to fear the rod, and to cry *softly*, by which means they escaped much correction which they might have had; and that most odious noise of the crying of children was never heard in the house.

During their one year of grace, the babies were trained into regular patterns of sleeping and eating by subtler and softer methods. Afterwards, Susanna adds:

They were taught to be still at family prayers, and to ask a blessing immediately after meals, which they used to do by signs before they could kneel or speak. They were quickly made to understand that they should have nothing they *cried for*, and instructed to speak respectfully for what they wanted.

From the first, they were made to observe the Sabbath and, as soon as they could speak, they were taught to say the Lord's Prayer morning and evening. As they grew, extra prayers and memorized Bible readings were added. By the time they were grown, they all knew vast tracts of the Bible, some of them whole books, by heart.

At mealtimes, the children sat at a small separate table and ate what they were given. Also, 'They were suffered to eat and drink as much as they would, but *not to call for anything*.' They were allowed nothing to eat or drink between meals and were beaten if they asked the kitchen staff for anything. They always addressed each other, not simply by name, but as 'Brother Charles' and so on.

The central principle behind Susanna's regime was the struggle against original sin. Children, she had good reason to believe, are born with a wicked rebellious will, which must be broken before any positive education can be attempted. This will is the root of all sin and misery, and the essence of Christianity is learning to submit it to God. What seemed cruel to the world was in fact merciful, forcing the children into goodness when they were at their most malleable, before they picked up habits that would make it harder: 'Break the will, if you will not damn the child.'

There was an unwritten constitution governing family discipline that Susanna recalled. The first rule was honesty. Whatever fault a child was guilty of, if they freely confessed they were not beaten. This may not be as liberal as it is usually taken to be, when one considers the second rule: 'That no sinful action, as lying, *pilfering*, disobedience, quarrelling, &c., should ever pass unpunished.' This suggests that the 'faults' of the first rule may only have covered unintentional failings. However, they were not to be beaten twice for the same offence. Any positive good deed should be rewarded, especially if it went against their inclinations. It should be judged by intention, however badly it was performed, 'and the child, with sweetness, directed how to do better for the future'. Personal property was inviolable and promises were binding, as was the giving or swapping of possessions. Girls were not to be put to chores until they had learned to read well.

Just how typical this child-rearing programme was of 18th-century educational policy is hard to say, as no one other than Susanna left such records. It is often thought to have been fairly mainstream. It seems to show the influence of John Locke, the premier philosopher of the age, whose bestseller *Some Thoughts on Education* taught the importance of bending children's will so that they learn to control their desires. However, this by no means indicates that most parents followed the principle with such rigour and Susanna was harsher than Locke in a number of ways. The isolationist aspects of Susanna's regime are not only unprecedented, but suggest that her strictness was not shared by other parents and so her children had to be insulated from others. On the other hand, her ways were not as extraordinary as they would be today, when they would bring social services to the door.

On his fifth birthday, John started lessons – as did they all, boys and girls. The school day was from nine to five, with a two-hour lunch break, and they were expected to learn the alphabet from start to finish on day one. Only Mary and Anne needed a second morning to get the hang of it, and Samuel had mastered it by lunchtime. This grasped, they were then set to reading the Bible, starting at the beginning and deciphering a verse at a time. The girls were educated far beyond the usual level for the 18th century.

In 1705, Samuel's propensity to debt and making enemies landed him in prison. He was a poor manager, perpetually failing to turn a profit from his estates, so, for people of their class, the Wesleys lived frugally. After five years at Epworth, he was in debt to one and a half times his annual income. There was an election in 1705, and Samuel promised his influential support to a local candidate, but changed his mind. Supporters of the disappointed candidate surrounded the rectory, beating drums and firing guns. One of them was owed £30 by him and now recalled it. As he could not pay, Samuel went to debtors' prison, where he stayed for several months until he had raised the money. Meanwhile, the house and his animals were repeatedly attacked.

So now, we have arrived back where we came in, with the fire of 1709. This had a disastrous effect on Susanna's regime. While the rectory was being rebuilt, the children were evacuated to various friends and neighbours and, when they returned home, Susanna was horrified by the change that had come over them. They had been allowed to talk to servants and play out with whomever they chose. Their Sabbath day routine had slackened. According to Susanna, they:

> … got knowledge of several songs and bad things, which before they had no notion of. That civil behaviour which made them admired when they were at home, by all who saw them, was in great measure lost; and a clownish accent, and many rude ways were learnt, which were not reformed without some difficulty.

We may be sure that Susanna was up to the job and set about it with a vengeance. (The complete collapse of Susanna's regime as soon as the children were borrowed by the outside world further challenges the idea that hers was a popular approach.)

It is now that the first glimpses of John's personality emerge from the general Wesleyishness of the rectory. It was at the age of six that, by his own recollection, he first became 'serious in religion'. He also emerges as a remarkably cerebral child, after his mother's image, with a propensity to analyse and deliberate over everything. 'As for Jack,' observed his father of John, 'he will have a reason for everything he has to do. I suppose he will not even break wind, unless he had a reason for it.'

When offered a snack, it was his habit to answer, 'I thank you; I will think of it.' He questioned, not so much out of a disinclination to obey, it seems, as from an assumption that there are logical reasons behind all human affairs and a desire to know what they were. His father tried to disillusion him: 'Child, you think to carry everything by dint of argument, but you will find how little is ever done in the world by close reasoning.' Throughout his life, the assumption that if he could give a logical argument for his actions he was justified in them, no matter what hurt he caused, was to be possibly Wesley's greatest weakness.

When he was eight, the rector judged that John was ready, in understanding and seriousness, for his first Communion. Soon after, he caught smallpox. He bore it bravely, like a man, and like a Christian, his mother said. He sometimes looked sourly at his spots, but never said anything.

About this time, an incident occurred with interesting echoes of John's future career. Samuel was away at Convocation again, and in his absence, Susanna, concerned at the family's missing out on the Sunday afternoon service, started devotions for them at home. She led in prayer and discussion and read sermons and the stories of the first Protestant missions that were now in circulation. Then some of the parish started joining them. Next thing we know, there were over 200 people crowding in.

Samuel's reaction was that of this conservative century in general – he warned her that such irregularity might seem scandalous and fanatical. His curate, understandably, was even more unhappy and complained that she was holding conventicles – the illegal gatherings of Dissenters. Her defence on this count was that, as the meeting brought 200 more of the parish into church, it was the opposite of a conventicle and stopping it now would hardly endear the curate to them. She was no more submissive to her husband's concerns about disrepute, replying that she scorned public opinion: 'I have long since shook hands with the world.' She had serious reservations about the propriety of leading prayers as a woman, but the success of the meetings and the parishioners' importunity persuaded her to continue until Samuel returned. Susanna's missed vocation is, sadly, unmistakable.

CHAPTER 3

THE WORLD: CHARTERHOUSE SCHOOL AND OLD JEFFERY (1714–20)

'Guilty Nature's Sleep'

From 'O for a thousand tongues to sing'

From this sheltered nest, John was suddenly ejected at the age of 10. In January 1714, he left Lincolnshire and was sent to Charterhouse School in London. This was the centenary year of the school, though the building had started life in 1371 as a monastery. John was awarded a free place as one of its few 'poor scholars', on the recommendation of Samuel's former patron, the Duke of Buckinghamshire.

His uniform included a black jacket, knee-length trousers, high collar and hat. The boys rose at five, but they got breakfast – bread, cheese and beer – at eight. (Beer was far cheaper than tea or coffee; the price of a pound of tea would have bought you 360 pots of ale.) John promised his father that before that time every day he would run three times round the garden. Supper was the same again, but the midday meal was more substantial. However, according to his later recollections, the social structure of public school entailed older boys taking all but his bread. At night, they slept two to a bed, which would have been no novelty to him.

Weekends and holidays he spent at his brother Samuel's, who, having graduated from Oxford and married, had now returned to his old school in Westminster as an usher. Jack was 'a brave boy', reported Samuel to their father, 'and learning Hebrew as fast as he can'.

Wesley was to look back on these years as his rebellious phase, though in most people's lives they would pass for a religious phase. He still read the Bible and said his prayers evening and morning, and his behaviour seems to have been exemplary. Nevertheless, in the harsh light of his evangelical conversion, he remembered this time as a fall from grace. Before going to school, he said in his *Journal*, 'I had not sinned away that "washing of the Holy Ghost" which was given me in baptism,' but now, flown from the intense regime of the family home and surrounded by worldly boys of his own age, he inevitably grew slacker in his spiritual life. While, before, he had sinned in thought, he now perpetually fell into sins of word and deed, of negligence as well as weakness. He was not specific in his recollections, but it is clear that we are talking of failings that generally went quite unnoticed as such by the world. While at home, he had been taught that he could be saved from hell by his strict obedience to the commandments of God, he now (he recalled) slackened his theology to fit and hoped to achieve this end by Bible reading, prayers and church attendance, by his feeling for religion and his not being as bad as other people. However, later still, he remembered the spirituality of his schooldays far more positively: 'I have not found God so present with me for so long a time since I was 12 years old.'

Apart from this loss of Eden, the most significant event of John's Charterhouse years was one in which he was not involved. At this point in the telling, Epworth Rectory gives us a ghost story. It starts on the night of 1 December 1716, when Anne and Susanna the younger heard an unusual knocking in the house. They told their sisters and mother and the noises repeated for them. Samuel's manservant Robert heard someone come 'slaring' through the garret into his room and alongside him. On other nights, they heard groans, breaking glass, doors slamming, the turning of a mill. Emily named the poltergeist 'Old Jeffery' after a man who had died in the house. Samuel alone was oblivious to his activity, and the family delayed telling him for two weeks: if the phenomena was genuinely supernatural, they would most likely be portents of death – presumably his. By the time Susanna told him, she was willing to believe the visitor was from the spirit world, but Samuel certainly was not. 'Sukey, I am ashamed of you,' he scolded, 'these boys and girls fright one another; but you are a woman of sense and should know better. Let me hear no more.'

He did hear more, however, and for himself. There were footsteps on the stairs, and the sound of dancing. There were rumblings, bangings and the gobbling of a turkey. The ghost echoed the girls' brushing and squeaked like some unknown animal. It did not limit its manifestations to noise alone, however. Jeffery lifted latches and threw open a door against Emily. Samuel and Susanna heard and felt a shower of coins on them in bed. Once, when Susanna investigated its scratchings under a bed, something 'pretty much like a badger' scuttled out, disappeared under Emily's skirts and was gone. Robert twice saw some such creature. The rector's mastiff at first barked at Old Jeffery, but as the haunting intensified, he whimpered in fear. The poltergeist was clearly politicized, making a particular point of disturbing Samuel's prayers for the king. Others outside the family also witnessed it, such as the vicar of nearby Haxby who came by to hear Old Jeffery's noises and had the presence of mind to try and shoot it.

Old Jeffery took a break in January, but returned on the 24th, starting again by interrupting Samuel's loyal prayer. At this point, he added to his usual tricks the repeated levitating of Anne's bed as she sat on it. They never once persuaded him to speak.

When Samuel did not die, worry shifted to Samuel junior in Westminster, from whom they had not heard in a surprisingly long time. However, he wrote soon enough. He was fascinated by Old Jeffery, eager to hear all they could tell him, and passed the stories on to an equally fascinated John. However, by now, the Wesleys' fear had long subsided into complacency, followed by irritation. 'I cannot imagine how you should be so curious about our unwelcome guest,' wrote his mother. 'For my part, I am quite tired with hearing or speaking of it.' Stung, perhaps, by this example of the human capacity for boredom, Old Jeffery suddenly disappeared and never returned.

What are we to make of Old Jeffery? The story is said to be one of the best authenticated stories of its kind ever by people who study them. Enough educated people witnessed the manifestations enough times to give it unusual credibility. Certainly, much of the story could be explained as hoax, much of the remainder as suggestibility and auto-suggestion and another part as being the tale growing in the telling. Nevertheless, even this still seems to leave us with something genuinely inexplicable.

The real point of the story, though, is that John was utterly convinced. He evidently had an innate taste for the supernatural and Old Jeffery brought it to the surface. Intrigued by his family's accounts, he later collected and published them. His own interpretation was that the visitations were demonic, sent to punish Samuel for his foolish vow to shun his wife, made 15 years earlier. His letters home often repeated other ghost stories he had heard. When he next went home, he wrote an account of the haunting from Samuel's diary and the family's recollections. Such credulity was rather out of step with educated society in the age of reason, which derided superstition, but Wesley was firm and, throughout his life, believed in ghosts, witches and demons. In later years, he was to welcome the paranormal manifestations his preaching provoked in a way that upset even his closest colleagues.

This, then, is the 16-year-old who now completes his school years and leaves London for Oxford University. We see an orderly, logical reasoner with a feel for the supernatural; a boy with a powerful attachment to his home and the ways of his family, neither of which he has seen (Samuel excluded) in many years; and a clever, hardworking child of unusual piety and moral standards, but with a consciousness, however vague, of having failed them.

CHAPTER 4

THE SPIRIT AND THE
FLESH: OXFORD
(1720–29)

**'Anticipate your Heaven below,
And own that Love is Heaven.'**
From 'O for a thousand tongues to sing'

John Wesley enrolled at Christ Church – the most illustrious college in Oxford, as his brother Samuel had before him, and his brother Charles would after him – on 24 June 1720, five days before his 17th birthday. The curriculum that all students followed was still at root medieval, training them in logic, rhetoric, morals and politics – the Aristotelean disciplines – and focusing on a selection of ancient writers, although the rationalistic philosophy of Locke and the science of Newton were starting to seep in. The university was enormously conservative, by intention: its raison d'être was to maintain and pass on a body of orthodox tradition and learning as it had for centuries. In many ways its system was outmoded and run down, lectures and exams having become half-hearted formalities. Wesley remembered them as 'an execrable insult upon the common sense' and 'an idle, useless interruption of useful studies'. It seems to have been easy enough to graduate without learning a great deal. A more familiar aspect of university life, maybe, was that students were widely suspected of being idle, drunken, privileged layabouts, though indulging in rather more fox-hunting than their modern counterparts. The strength of Oxford was in its tutorial system – Wesley's tutors were learned, conscientious and capable teachers with whom he got on very well.

He worked as hard as ever and did well, though he still castigated himself for idleness. This was probably because he had such a full social life – tennis and billiards, boating and walks, chess and cards, dances, theatre and coffee houses. He wrote romantic Latin verse and read widely – poetry and plays, history and theology.

He seemed to be inheriting his father's propensity to debt. He had £20 a year from Charterhouse and got a scholarship from Christ Church, but repeatedly had to borrow from friends, including his tutor. From 1722, his parents were able to help him out a little better, as Samuel was given the living of nearby Wroot in addition to Epworth. Still, in his fourth year, telling his mother the story of a friend's being robbed of his hat and wig in the street, he was able to add, 'I am pretty safe from such gentlemen; for unless they carried me away, carcass and all, they would have but a poor purchase.'

He wore no wig and his hair long to save on barbers. Such frugality stayed with him for the rest of his life, even when he had a handsome income as, what he took to as an economic necessity, he continued as a spiritual discipline.

After graduating in 1724, Wesley stayed on at Christ Church to study for his Masters degree. We are coming now to a major turning point in his life, a spiritual awakening where he came to take his faith more seriously than ever before, wrestling with religious discipline, theology and his hormones.

An early manifestation of this came with his reading, in November 1724, of a book entitled *Health and Long Life* by one Dr Cheyne. The doctor prescribed a regimen of strict moderation in food and drink, supported by sleep and good exercise. Wesley had had small opportunity for anything other than moderation so far in his life, but he responded to the book with great enthusiasm, and it shaped his thinking for the rest of his life. Between now and his evangelical conversion, he was to develop an ever more austerely ascetic spirituality, but even after that, the value of self-discipline and a simple lifestyle would always be of the utmost importance for him.

A profound, though less tangible, impact came from the question of what the young graduate was going to do with his life. For men of his background, with an education but no capital, choice of career tended to be restricted to the priesthood and education. As most teachers were men of the cloth anyway, ordination was clearly a natural step. The qualifications for it were minimal and a sense of special calling was as unnecessary then as it would be for a career in banking today.

Nevertheless, Wesley took the decision seriously and had doubts about taking up such great work. Samuel reassured him, plainly considering it a question of when, not whether or not. His mother was already dropping none too subtle hints about how good it would be for him to come back home as his father's curate. She pushed John to be ordained by Easter, so that he could start gaining practical experience, but Samuel told him to wait because he wanted him to help with editing a polyglot Bible, which work would provide exactly the right preparation for holy orders. Again, we see the difference in temperament between husband and wife, the practical versus the bookish. ''Tis an unhappiness almost peculiar to our family,' sighed Susanna, rather unrealistically, 'that your father and I seldom think alike.' In fact, Samuel soon came round to Susanna's way of thinking, but as it turned out, it was not possible for John to be ordained until September.

In the meantime, encouraged by his mother, and, it seems, by the prospect of an impending vocation for which he felt unprepared, he examined the state of his soul, weighing up, as she instructed, 'whether you have a reasonable hope of salvation'.

With this in view, he read Thomas à Kempis's *Of the Imitation of Christ* and Jeremy Taylor's *Rules and Exercises of Holy Living and Dying*. He was inspired, but had reservations about both. He could not accept à Kempis's assumption that all enjoyment of this life is an evil to be shunned, on the twin grounds that God created this life as much as the next and that it is just too plain gloomy to be taken seriously. As for the avalanche of laws that makes up Taylor's works, Wesley judged many of them simply unrealistic, and therefore harmful in undermining one's confidence in salvation.

Encouraged by his parents' partial agreement in this, John went on to sort out predestination. He felt a natural revulsion for the idea, as he thought it an affront both to God's goodness and human responsibility for one's actions, but could not escape the fact that it was upheld in the Thirty-Nine Articles. He toyed with the compromise that, although God predestines that some will be saved, it is our free choice whether or not we will be of that number. Failing to square that with the Articles, though, he decided instead that God elects certain people to salvation and the remainder are left with a free choice of whether or not they will be saved. This conclusion, abstract as it is, was to have untold ramifications for the history of the Methodist revival.

Two things stand out in these theological ruminations. The first is that when he explored his ideas in letters home, now as later, it was almost entirely with his mother. Samuel, noticing this, offered to answer any doubts his son had, but it seems that Susanna – whether for her mind or manner or both – was the preferred doctrinal authority.

The second curiosity lies in what unites those theological ideas Wesley had a problem with – ones expressing pessimism about humanity. There is a distinct impression in these early letters of a young man, serious, temperate and pious, but with a love of life and a heart in revolt against any dogmatic attempt to dampen or condemn that zest.

The fact is that Wesley was in love, or something quite like it. The girl in question was Sally Kirkham, a resident of the charming Cotswold village of Stanton. Her family was the centre of a circle of friends in the area that Wesley had joined thanks to Oxford connections and often visited. Their delightful cultured society was straight out of a Jane Austen novel, full of picnics, dances, the latest literature and witty, erudite conversation, though, of course, the people were dressed in somewhat earlier fashions. They were spiritual people too, discussing theology and enjoying Wesley's sermons. It was quite possibly Sally who first put him on to – and off – Jeremy Taylor and his rule books.

There was no question of them marrying in the foreseeable future. It would be a matter of years before Wesley could support a family and he was deeper in debt than ever. They seem, however, to have been happy to keep their relationship on an almost flirtatious level, their energies sublimated into shared spiritual passions, each finding that their conversations roused them to greater holy fervour. They called each other, as was the odd custom of this social circle, by literary nicknames: she was Varanese and he Cyrus.

Romance was a pursuit in which few of Wesley's family had ever found happiness, but 1725 was certainly a year for it, a time to embrace and a time to refrain from embracing. First was Emily, his eldest sister, to whom John was especially close. She had had a long-standing attachment to a university friend of the boys called Robert Leybourne, but when they announced their intention to marry, her brother Samuel and her mother forbade them and Leybourne decided not to push it. Emily was 33. In April 1725, she wrote a crushed letter to John saying 'if my advice is worth listening to, never engage your affections before your worldly affairs are in such a posture that you may marry very soon'. He received it days before he first met Sally. After a miserable spell as an exploited teacher in Lincoln, Emily admitted defeat by the outside world and returned to the rectory where she believed herself duty bound to attend her mother.

Susanna, the next sister, had married a rich farmer called Richard Ellison, but he proved coarse by Wesley standards, and morose and brutal by any. Having borne several children, she left him and returned to the rectory.

Hetty, meanwhile, was in love with a local lawyer by the name of Will Attkins. The most vivacious, intelligent, accomplished and witty of the sisters (and the first suspect of hoax in the Old Jeffery mystery), she had always been a source of anxiety for her parents, whether fairly or not. Samuel's comment, 'I've had little hopes of her... since she has been a year and a half old,' suggests a self-fulfilling prophecy. It was Samuel who had stood in the way of this marriage and, though Hetty was ready to elope, Attkins called it off. The subsequent events are unclear, but it seems she got into another relationship and was found out. On 1 August 1725, she eloped, presumably already pregnant as she had a child the following February. Ten weeks after the elopement, she married William Wright, a plumber. It is usually supposed that Samuel forced her into this marriage to cover up her pregnancy, though the evidence suggests rather that she married him to spite her father, who utterly disowned her from the day of her elopement and does not come out of the scandal well. 'Gangrene, farewell!' was his considered reflection on his daughter's leaving. 'She is lost to me,' he told John, though 'not so well as dead'. He refused to speak to her ever again. The baby died in its first year, the couple moved to Soho and Hetty was destroyed by a wretched, heartless marriage.

There were two further marriages before the year was out. Anne Wesley married a land surveyor named John Lambert in December 1725 and their union was uncharacteristically happy. The same month, Sally, John's beloved, married Reverend John Chapone. Wesley was stoical: 'May God give her all the happiness she deserves.'

The year 1725 also saw Wesley getting to grips with his faith, not only intellectually but practically. Longing for a new level of holiness in his life, he worked at a programme of self-discipline, writing himself rules to live by: how and how not to spend his time, the kind of company to avoid and attitudes to foster. His general rule was, 'Whenever you are to do an action, consider how Christ did or would do the like and you are to imitate his example.'

Despite his earlier reservations about Taylor, it was he who inspired him to start a diary. There he examined his conduct of the day, as well as noting new resolutions and writing prayers for help. The day after his ordination in September, he pledged to examine himself twice daily. He particularly struggled with what he saw as laziness, resolving to fill all his spare time with religion, setting out a methodical study timetable and aiming to rise at five every morning.

He started taking more seriously the danger of 'idle pleasures', an idea that was to be key to his spirituality. While Epworth had taught him to shun sinful pleasures that corrupt the soul, in favour of virtuous pursuits that edify it, this had left plenty of room for diversions that are neither one nor the other, such as dancing and games. However, Wesley was starting to pursue this to its logical conclusion. In the struggle for his soul, if an idle pleasure diverted him from spiritual edification, then, however innocent it was in itself, it had become a sin. To the mature Wesley, any activity that was not positively serving God was a moral failure: 'Of those things which are lawful in themselves, such only are lawful to me as are conducive either directly or indirectly to my holiness or usefulness.'

In 1726, Wesley was elected to an Oxford Fellowship. This was a recognition of his character and academic ability and also the result of his father's political record and lobbying for Wesley. He became a Fellow of Lincoln College on 17 March. The college's Lincolnshire connections were useful in securing the Fellowship, particularly the fact that the retiring Fellow was a relation of the MP that Samuel ensured was elected in 1705.

The Fellowship at last meant financial security for Wesley. It came with a sizeable allowance and free rooms, which he could rent out when he was not using them. His duties in return included lecturing (in logic, Greek and philosophy) and the pastoral care of students. It was by no means a full-time occupation and left him free to spend long spells at home as his father's curate, helping him with his latest project – a huge, learned commentary on Job.

His spiritual self-exploration continued and the change of college gave a new spur to his efforts at self-improvement. Wesley recalls:

> I executed a resolution which I was before convinced was of the utmost importance, shaking off at once all trifling acquaintance. I began to see more and more the value of time. I applied myself closer to study. I watched more carefully against actual sins; I advised others to be religious, according to that scheme of religion by which I modelled my life.

As well as the flight from idle pleasures and the compulsion to make use of every moment, the separatist ethos of the rectory seems to be reasserting itself here, Wesley feeling the need to cut himself off from former friends for the sake of his soul. Another essential Wesleyism: he has no shyness at all about taking responsibility for others' spiritual lives as he took responsibility for his own.

He told his brother Samuel, 'Leisure and I have taken leave of one another: I propose to be busy as long as I live.' Though this perfectly describes his later life, for the present his doing lagged behind his intention. The diary continued to pick over his daily failings – above all that of wasting time in activities such as light reading and oversleeping, arguing too heatedly, intellectual dishonesty, impure thoughts and putting people down. Alongside these sit notes on how to do the latest dances and some pretty worldly verses, but Wesley was developing an ever more uncomfortable dissonance in his spiritual life – a conflict between the worldly and the godly. It seems à Kempis was getting through.

One would assume that the loss of Sally had at least a part in this sudden transformation, but extraordinarily enough, they carried on much as ever. In fact, if anything, their relationship intensified after her marriage. He would hold her hand and lie on her breast while she said 'many obliging things'. 'Methinks 'tis almost a sin', she declared, 'to prostitute those expressions of tenderness to others which I have at any time applied to you. I can't think it expedient nor indeed lawful to break off that acquaintance which is one of the strongest incentives I have to virtue.' 'I would certainly acquit you if my husband should ever resent our freedom but the esteem I have to you… as it is grounded on reason and virtue… no circumstance of life shall ever make me alter.' He enthused to his mother about their friendship, but she was cautious: she hoped their conversation would prove innocent and useful, 'but old folks are scrupulous and fear the consequences'.

By then, another romantic tumult had hit Wesley's life. This time it was an Epworth girl called Kitty Hargreaves, whom he saw a lot over the summer. The hawk-eyed rector soon picked up on it and sent her away. John's conscience took his father's side and he struggled with his desire. 'As we would willingly suffer a little pain, or forgo some pleasure for others we really love, so if we sincerely love God we should readily do this for him,' he wrote in his diary. 'Begin in small things first,' he resolved. 'Never touch Kitty's hand again.' However, it seems that the flesh was weak – or too strong – for not only did he see her repeatedly over the coming weeks, but was adding to his resolution a month later 'never to touch a woman's breasts again'.

The greatest storm of the summer, though, was one that John created himself for the sake of his sister Hetty – an incident that shows him to be strong on charity and hugely lacking in tact. The family still shunned her for her lack of chastity, despite protestations of repentance, which they reckoned were false, and John decided enough was enough. He hardly chose the most direct way of challenging them:

he preached a sermon on charity in his father's church in Wroot, teaching the congregation what learned divines had said about forgiveness and happened to add in the last paragraph that his father's treatment of his sister was an excellent example of how not to do it. As Susanna observed, 'You writ this sermon for Hetty; the rest was brought in for the sake of the last paragraph.'

The rector was of course outraged and the rest of the family shocked. John affected to be amazed at having caused offence, but apologized to Samuel and promised never to contradict him again. There were tears and kisses and all was resolved, until the next service, when John did the same thing with a sermon on rash judging. This time it was months before they could be reconciled.

CHAPTER 5

THE PURSUIT OF HOLINESS
(1729–30)

'Pure and spotless let us be.'
From 'Love divine, all loves excelling'

A momentous change had come over Wesley, but from zealous ordinand to evangelical field-preacher – and from personal reformation to international revival – was a long and tortured journey. The first step was a small and inauspicious one in 1729 – he was recalled to tutorial duties at Oxford.

The story starts with his brother Charles, who came up to Christ Church in January 1727. If we can take his later evangelical testimony at face value, he took the chance to throw off the restraints of Wesley family life and 'slept in the arms of Satan'. However, we cannot, as the fact is that he did little work in his first year and had a mild romance with a London actress called Molly, who apparently found him terribly naive, and that seems to be it. He had never been interested in anything more than nominal religion, and when John raised the subject, he snapped, 'What would you have me a saint all at once?'

After a year in Oxford, though, Charles became far more spiritual – a change he put down, significantly, to his mother's prayers. His efforts to live out his faith were not at first completely successful – a fact he attributed to the godlessness of Christ Church, 'the worst place on earth to begin a reformation in' – but he had encouragement from John. He threw himself into his studies and took Communion every week instead of the once-a-term minimum that most students contented themselves with.

Having started to get to grips with his own spiritual life, Charles lost no time in taking responsibility for others'. He was close friends with Bob Kirkham, Sally's brother, and constantly badgered him (with no discernible effect) to spend more time in study. More successfully, he took a young neighbour by the name of William Morgan under his wing and persuaded him to renounce all his friends other than Charles himself and Bob; he also had him taking weekly Communion. Charles applied himself to his studies, working methodically through the official reading recommended by the university. The three of them met together now and again so that they could encourage each other (or be encouraged by Charles) to do likewise.

This virtuous clique was not popular among the students. A weekly sacrament smacked of fanaticism and, less than a century after religious fanatics had overthrown the monarchy, popular opinion was not going to tolerate that kind of thing. University authorities, however, shared some of Charles's dismay about his fellow students. They were concerned about their moral and religious laxity and alarmed by the small but growing number who were being seduced by the fashionable new heresies of Arianism (which denied the deity of Christ) and Deism (which denied most other doctrines too on the grounds that God does not intervene to communicate with humanity). More supervision was required, and the Heads of Houses started recalling tutors to ensure the oversight of students in person.

Thus it was that the letter went out to John on 21 October 1729, summoning him back to Lincoln College to lecture and tutor, supervise 11 students and minister in a nearby parish. When he came, he joined Charles's holy circle and soon became its dominant personality. Their meetings increased to three or four a week and they also ate and prayed together. Maybe it was John's influence that finally persuaded Bob Kirkham to go for a Wesley-style reformation. He gave up tea for breakfast and social drinking of an evening and studied all day.

Wesley's responsibilities for his students being moral as well as academic, he imposed his own regime on them with alacrity. For example, he not only told them which books to read, but forbade them to read any others. At the same time, he grew ever stricter on himself, writing a new self-catechism to review not only his daily deeds but also if his motives were sufficiently directed to the glory of God. He discouraged visitors to his room who might waste his time, and abandoned such frivolities as cards and dancing.

With his personal regime becoming ever stricter, Wesley chose this moment to embark on another intense female relationship. Mrs Mary Pendarves was a wealthy 30-year-old widow who had been part of the Kirkham circle in the Cotswolds. It was probably she who had started their tradition of calling each other by literary pseudonyms, though she also had another nickname for him – 'Primitive Christianity' – a first indication of his lifelong preoccupation with recapturing the life of the early Church. His letters to Mary read somewhat artificially, full of flattery, overblown language and the praise of virtue. It was a rather one-sided relationship – her letters were shorter, less frequent and less effusive than his. The affair was less romantic than the one with Sally and quite consciously in its shadow: he would gush about 'that soft emotion with which I glow even at the moment while I consider myself conversing with a kindred spirit of my Varanese'.

One wonders what went on in Wesley's mind concerning these relationships. He had similar though less intense involvement with sisters of both Mary and Sally, where spiritual mentoring and romantic passions got sometimes painfully entangled. Consciously, Wesley saw these as matters of mutual spiritual edification. It is tempting to play this down and explain their religious concerns as a mask for romantic indulgence and a channel for superfluous sexual energy. Doubtless this was a part of it – Wesley clearly relished female company for its own sake – but it is equally clear that he relished the opportunity to give advice and encouragement and that this, just like the Holy Club, was the outlet for a deep desire to pastor. As for mutual edification, one suspects that the greater part of the edification Wesley received from the relationships was the opportunity to edify.

Meanwhile back at the Holy Club, a crucial new development took place. For no discernible reason, William Morgan decided to pop into Oxford Castle prison and see a murderer. He was shocked by the conditions there, with mere debtors crammed in with killers. He got talking to a man who was there for debt and took the opportunity to offer him some spiritual encouragement, to which he was receptive. He started going frequently to talk to prisoners and enthused to his friends about how much good he was able to do for them.

On 24 August, the Wesley brothers went with him and were impressed. They had themselves a calling. They decided to work a couple of regular visits into their weekly programme. You can imagine the response this brought from those who already made fun of the 'Saints' for studying and praying. It was enough to make John write to his father and ask if he thought that this venture was going too far. Samuel's answer was a surprise: he not only approved (with all the violence that he usually directed at things he approved and disapproved of, talking of adopting William Morgan as his son), but revealed that he had done the very same thing as an undergraduate in Oxford himself. On Samuel's advice, John applied to the Bishop of Oxford for permission. The bishop was enthusiastic about the project too, and let him not only visit but preach to his captive audience.

It is an exaggeration to say, as it has been, that this was Wesley's turning outwards from his earlier self-absorbed religion. Not only do his letters to Mary exemplify a long-standing desire to better others, but also his obsessive self-examination continued to intensify. Still, there is some truth in the idea, as now Wesley had a better outlet for his pastoral inclinations than ever before, and he became increasingly concerned with helping others.

In the meantime, Morgan had found another new avenue for the Holy Club's goodwill. On 31 August, he took Wesley to visit a local woman who was ill, and the experience persuaded them to include such visits each week. They put their money where their faith was, starting a small fund so that they could give some more material encouragement to those they visited.

The little company started growing, and armchair supporters who did not fancy joining in their activities gave donations to their funds instead. Naturally, the name-calling increased: 'the Saints Club', 'the Holy Company', 'the Biblemoths'. Who called whom what and when is unclear. Charles gives the impression that his methodical study group had already received the choicest nomenclature before John arrived;

John suggested that it only started coming when his strict spiritual method was becoming well known. Either way, they were now 'the Methodists'. Wesley felt the criticism strongly enough to write a defence of their 'little company', which consisted entirely of rhetorical questions: 'Whether... we may not try to do good to those that are hungry, naked, or sick?'

Their most influential opposition came from the Canon of Christ Church. When he found that the nephew who lived with him had joined and was taking weekly Communion, he threatened to throw him out. When that failed, he tried strangulation. Then he turned to gentle persuasion and finally convinced the boy of the perils of too much sacrament. The canon arranged a meeting of college authorities to discuss how to combat this fanaticism. Rumour said that they planned 'to blow up the Godly Club', but nothing seems to have come of this.

CHAPTER 6

THE HOTTER PURSUIT OF HOLINESS (1731–35)

'Wrestle and fight and pray'
From 'Soldiers of Christ, arise'

In 1731, the Holy Club more or less collapsed when the Wesleys went back to Epworth for the summer. Bob Kirkham left to become his uncle's curate and William Morgan was very ill. However, on his return, John managed to ensure that things were happening again and a number of new recruits joined in. The work gave a new focus to his spirituality as his struggles against idleness were more successful now he actually had something to do with his time. He was at last regularly getting up at five (which also conquered the insomnia that had been troubling him for years), and increasingly withdrawing from Oxford society.

In November 1731, Wesley had a discussion with his brother Samuel that offers quite an insight in to the way he was coming to be seen by others and himself. Samuel was anxious: reports that reached him about John suggested he was taking his religion to unnecessary extremes. The pursuit of holiness was commendable, but was he laying excessive burdens on himself that were liable to injure his health? Samuel was not sorry to hear that he was rising early and keeping out of company, but was sorry to hear him described as singular, whimsical and overly formal. Being prone to consumption, he should sit by the fire and have his hair cut. Was long hair scriptural anyway?

John observed that, as they agreed on the pursuit of holiness and a well-regulated life, the only question between them was one of means. They agreed that his insularity and early rising (which required an equally unsociable bedtime) were appropriate means, but these were the very things that annoyed people into complaining about his other habits. As to the excessive burdens of his religious regime, he was compelled in the pursuit of holiness to do anything that worked, and what worked for him only he could judge. Those who warned him of excess simply put stumbling blocks in his way – which is what all with his aims should expect. 'Singular'? Yes, he was different from others, but not without reason. 'Formal'? Yes, he lacked a genteel sociable manner; so what? 'Serious'? Also true: 'Mirth, I grant, is fit for you; but does it follow that it is fit for me?' Should John not rejoice that the enemy was conquered and that he had passed from death to life? That would indeed be grounds for rejoicing, but the enemy was not defeated, he attacked daily, and as for his eternal salvation, he lived in constant fear and struggle. With regard to biblical hair, the money he saved on it went – he hinted – to those in need, and was not that more biblical than any hairstyle?

Samuel was mortified to hear that he was a stumbling block to his brother's salvation. He had not meant to set his spirituality up as a model for John, but instead was worried about those who would take John's own rigour as a model. John, likewise, was upset to hear that Samuel had so understood him. The debate concluded with a touching note from Samuel asking John just to take care of his health:

> Your life is of benefit and consequence to the world, and I would therefore willingly, for the sake of others, draw your days out to the utmost date. For yourself indeed the matter is not much, if you will go well whensoever you are called; as I don't question but you will. As to any faults I have to tell you of... the main is what I have often repeated – your soul is too great for your body.

Samuel's worries about Wesley's example could not have been more ominously timed. In February 1732, William Morgan, who had been seriously ill for months, delivered the Holy Club its worst blow yet by losing his mind. For the time being he stayed in Oxford, where Wesley continued to regale him with his mother's deliberations on the real presence of Christ in the Eucharist.

Morgan's father was furious with 'that ridiculous society', blaming its excesses for his son's decline, and refusing him any further financial allowance except to cover his health and education. When he first became ill the previous year, Wesley's protégé had been 'exceeding well pleased with the thoughts of dying shortly', but now that he was at heaven's door he lost his confidence and could not bear to hear talk of the subject. He returned home to Dublin, but the doctors sent him back to Oxford for better air. On the journey, he was scared by hallucinations and drove his horse all round the countryside, attacking the servant who tried to help, saying that God would guide him. Returning home, he was locked up by his father, according to whom he repeatedly cried, 'O religious madness,' blaming his fanaticism for his breakdown and trying to throw himself out of a high window in order to be with God. On 26 August, William Morgan died.

The most astonishing twist to the tale, however, is that 10 days later, Mr Morgan was writing to Charles saying that he had changed his mind about the Holy Club and wanted to help it in any way he could. Also, a year later, he entrusted his remaining son, Richard, to John's capable tutoring. Grief works in mysterious ways and Morgan clearly found solace in the thought that William's godliness must have secured him an eternal reward. However, these accounts of William's last ragings come from Mr Morgan's later attempts to persuade Wesley to go easy on Richard, so a little exaggeration might have been called for to make his point.

The word around Oxford, not surprisingly, was that Methodism had killed William Morgan. More surprising was Wesley's reaction. Eight months after William's death, Wesley responded to this criticism with a blisteringly insensitive letter to Mr Morgan, sarcastically rebutting the idea of his responsibility while insisting that he cared nothing for any man's opinion of him anyway. However unfortunate this letter, it has the virtue of preserving for biographers Wesley's account of the origins of the Holy Club.

Opposition intensified and, in December, a newspaper called *Fog's Journal* published a highly critical piece attacking their insane fanaticism. Suspicions were not eased when it became known that Wesley had extended his help to a man in prison for homosexuality. Not a man inclined to compromise, Wesley responded to his critics with a sermon on holiness at the university on 1 January 1733. He not only insisted on the vital importance of pursuing the call to holiness without restraint, but proclaimed for the first time the doctrine that was to prove his most singular and, in some ways, his most controversial – entire sanctification or perfection. Taking the text 'Circumcision is that of the heart', he defined this circumcision as a state of acceptance by God consisting not only in the forgiveness of sins but 'the being so "renewed in the spirit of our mind", as to be "perfect as our Father in heaven is perfect"'. A year previously, he had been happy to say 'our hope is sincerity, not perfection'; that was, to say the least, no longer the whole story.

As his goals were elevated, his self-analysis and self-discipline were turning into obsessions that those who enjoyed Methodist-baiting would have rejoiced in. He now updated his spiritual audit on an hourly basis and not only noted his successes and failures, but gave himself a score out of nine. 'My desire', he told Susanna, 'is to know and feel that I am nothing, that I have nothing, and that I can do nothing.'

In June, John was 30. He was away from Oxford in Manchester for a month in the summer, saving money by going both ways on foot. (Susanna's rebuking him and Charles for saving money by not eating on the road had evidently fallen on deaf ears.) Once again, the Holy Club collapsed in his absence. He returned to find numbers at Monday Communion reduced by over 80 per cent. His college pupils were protesting against the 'singularity' he demanded, such as fasting on Wednesdays. His response was to stop staying away from Oxford.

Recruits continued to come, and one of 1733's newcomers was to prove one of the most important friendships of Wesley's life. A 19-year-old student at Pembroke College, who had been raised at the Bell Inn, Gloucester, George Whitefield had heard of the Holy Club before coming to Oxford, and, 11 years John's junior, he worshipped the

Wesleys from afar. He followed their rule of life rigidly and nearly starved. Now he finally made star-struck contact.

It was also now that Mr Morgan sent Richard to Lincoln College under John's tuition. He arrived with a greyhound, which was against college rules 'An ill prospect', judged Wesley. Mr Morgan pleaded that Richard be spared the Holy Club; John assured him that there was no danger of their accepting one 'so little experienced in piety or charity'.

Then, on 14 January 1734, Wesley went into Richard's room, saw a letter to Mr Morgan complaining bitterly about the Methodist principles that his tutor expected him to live by, and he read it. Richard had written an exaggerated account of their activities, claiming in addition to the truth that they would 'endeavour to reform notorious whores, and allay spirits in haunted houses'. They were 'a frightful sight', emaciated by fasting. Wesley forbade him any company but their own, so he was forced to attend their meetings: an hour each night they would read requests for help from the poor and make plans for the coming day; the next hour they would hear and discuss a pious reading and they would then finish in prayer. They would often cry at length for their sins and then, thanking God for his gift of repentance, 'laugh immoderately as if they were mad' – this sounds suspiciously like the first hint of the charismatic phenomena that were to surround Wesley throughout his life. Richard complained that he had learned nothing but religion from his tutor. The Methodists were 'the jest of the university' and he suffered by association, 'for what they reckon the greatest happiness, namely of being laughed at, to me is the greatest misery'. In short, he wanted to change tutor.

Wesley's reaction, typically, was to write Mr Morgan an uncompromising, reasoned defence of his approach: he had been asked to lead Richard in a sober, religious life, but religion was not, as Mr Morgan supposed, merely a matter of saying your prayers and avoiding deliberate sins; it was about being remade in the divine image, an ever-increasing conformity to the heart and life of Christ. How could there possibly be such a thing as going too far or too fast in such a glorious enterprise? He also suggested that Richard's complaints were simply a ploy to discredit Wesley in case he should ever get a bad report.

Mr Morgan's reply was surprisingly mild and reasonable. Yes, Wesley argued most logically for his policy, but his episcopal friends agreed that it was a dangerous experiment for young men such as Richard. Either way, it was extraordinary that Wesley has proceeded in it when he was clearly asked by a bereaved father to keep Richard out of the Holy Club and go easy on him. Yet Morgan insisted, 'I respect and adore both you and every gentleman of that strict religious society that you are engaged in, and doubt not but you will meet with an exalted seat in heaven.' After writing, he told Richard to obey his tutor in everything and get rid of the dog.

Wesley's reply was pretty unpleasant. Uncompromising as ever, he simply used the whole of his rhetorical power to insist that his approach was right, that the fate of Richard's immortal soul was at stake and, with the truth of God on his side, Wesley had no business listening to human opinion. The letter does, on the other hand, do Wesley the credit of showing us that his control of Richard and others like him was not simply megalomania, but driven by the same compulsion to save his soul, whatever the cost, that was driving his own regime, which he extended in compassion for others.

The correspondence with Mary Pendarves had long tailed off due to her lack of interest, after being continued awhile single-handedly by an imploring John. However, she now wrote out of the blue, offering to renew their profitable friendship, but Wesley replied with a short, miserable note saying that recent experience showed he had not the power to profit anyone and she had proved she was no exception.

Samuel Wesley senior was dying. He had been seriously ill, suffered debilitating falls and, by the end of 1734, he was on his deathbed. He and the family urged John to take the rector's post, but he resolutely refused: his place was at Oxford. The family said he would do good for more people at Epworth than at Oxford. John replied candidly, 'The question is not whether I could do more good to others... but whether I could do more good to myself' – adding that 'wherever I can be most holy myself, there, I can most promote holiness in others'.

The dispute uncovers a vein of selfishness in Wesley's quest for sanctity that Samuel picked up on. Holiness was not something to cultivate in seclusion, he argued, one's light shining 'barely through the chinks of a bushel, for fear the wind should blow it out'. John replied, with a vast 5,000-word thesis of a letter, as uncompromising and logically bulldozing as ever. It revealed something like an addiction for Methodist persecution: 'Till be he thus contemned, no man is in a state of salvation.' As biographer Stanley Ayling comments:

> What Wesley is really saying, behind all the letter's long sermonizing and bandying of texts, is that he cannot accept a life of day-by-day contact with ordinary people. He hungers for righteousness, and to be persecuted for righteousness' sake, but not amid Epworth's humdrum acres, with their 2,000 souls, their 'trifling acquaintance' and 'impertinent company'.

The impression that Wesley is being profoundly dishonest with himself about his reasons for not wanting to take on Epworth was confirmed by the fact that, within a year, he had quit Oxford.

Samuel Wesley senior died in April 1735, with John and Charles at his bedside. Laying his hand on Charles's head he said, 'Be steady. The Christian faith shall surely revive in this kingdom; you shall see it, though I shall not.' And he told Emily, 'Do not be concerned at my death; God will then begin to manifest himself to my family.' John finally agreed to apply for the post, but was too late. Susanna moved out of the rectory and spent her remaining years in the houses of her children. Emily and Martha were hastily married. Emily wed an impoverished local apothecary with John (who had recently alienated his most devoted sister with an ill-informed criticism of her spiritual life) officiating. Providence seemed kinder to Martha, for the time being. She married Westley Hall, the brightest star of the Holy Club. Every day, gushed Wesley, he seems to have achieved all the holiness possible in one life, but every evening he has gone unimaginably further. 'O may I be a follower of him as he is of Christ!' He was to become a leading Methodist preacher and, after a string of seductions among his flock, turn to a gospel of polygamous deism, finally deserting Martha after most of her 10 children had died and taking another woman to the West Indies.

Wesley spent the summer putting the finishing touches to the vast learned commentary on Job to which his father had devoted the last 10 years of his life. He officially presented it to Queen Caroline who proclaimed it 'very prettily bound' and put it aside unopened. This was probably the kindest review the book received. Bishop Warburton likened it to Job having his brains sucked out by owls.

In the meantime, Wesley had been contacted by the Society for the Promotion of Christian Knowledge. It was looking for new ministers for Georgia, the three-year-old British settlement in America, to assist with public order and morals, and convert the natives. A whole new life beckoned to Wesley, a new start and a new hope in the new world. He persuaded Charles and Westley Hall to join him, gave optimistically strict instructions on how the remainder of the Holy Club were to conduct themselves and, the day after visiting the Queen, he was embarking on the *Simmonds*.

Chapter 7

The Wilderness: Georgia (1735–37)

'While the Tempest still is high'
From 'Jesu, lover of my soul'

Wesley's motive for going to Georgia was simple: to save his soul. In the back-to-basics society of the settlement, away from the demands of modern life and the distractions of womankind, he would have a chance to pursue the goal that eluded him in Oxford: the unhampered practice of holiness and the holy moulding of others. It was an unmitigated catastrophe.

The traditional evangelical understanding of Wesley's Oxford and Georgia years, including Wesley's own after his conversion, is that he was attempting salvation by works – saving one's soul by being holy enough to satisfy God's standards. In this instance, this book throws its negligible weight behind that school of thought. Admittedly, such accounts have sometimes been overly simplistic, as if these years were an unsatisfying struggle to appease God with mere outward observances. Wesley was most definitely grappling with his innermost soul, pursuing rebirth in the likeness of Christ, and his works were consciously dependent on Christ's prior work. It was the all-consuming pursuit of an ever-receding grail, but there is good reason to think that, in the earlier days at least, he found a measure of consolation in the chase.

Whatever the case, of the means to that salvation there was no doubt: to change his behaviour as far as lay in his power into the perfection of Christ. Behind everything that has happened in the last two chapters lay one simple motive: Wesley had a soul and it needed to be saved. Salvation comes in the struggle towards holiness.

The gospel he took to America could hardly be more different from the one to which he would devote his life after his return. Luther's liberating idea of justification by faith – saving one's soul merely by accepting God's offer of forgiveness – had been buried under two centuries of rubble, but now suddenly, across the English-speaking world, it was rising again with astonishing power. In 1734, at the other end of the British colonial coastline from that to which Wesley was going, Jonathan Edwards had sparked off a revival in New England with a sermon on justification by faith that eventually converted the entire town of 300 souls and spread throughout the region. The following year, two Welshmen – Howel Harris and Daniel Rowland – experienced evangelical conversions. These happened independently of Edwards and, indeed, of each other. The experience of God's forgiveness sent them into a punishing preaching tour, calling the country to repentance, and the response was huge. At the same time and again independently, George Whitefield was converted by a combination of Holy Club reading material and a deliverance simultaneously from fasting-induced illness and from 'unspeakable' temptation.

Untouched by any of this, John was accompanied to America by two of the Holy Club, Charles Delamotte and Benjamin Ingham, as well as by his brother (but not by Westley and Martha Hall, as Westley had backed out at the last minute). He had persuaded Charles most reluctantly to be ordained for the occasion and, as the ship waited for a good wind at Cowes, Charles was called on to preach four times in the parish church. Here he got an early taste of mass evangelism as crowds of the lower classes flocked to hear him and take away improving books. The Lieutenant Governor of Georgia, General James Oglethorpe, sailed with them.

They finally left English shores in November 1735. For John, the journey was one of terrors, doubt and ever more intense ascetic experiments. The four of them followed a strict timetable: two hours a day in private prayer, two hours leading public prayers, two hours in Bible study, two hour-long meetings to report on their successes and failures and plan ahead, then an hour reading to a small group of passengers. Wesley also spent three hours a day learning German to converse with the 26 German Pietists on board, and an hour at their service – a 13-hour total. It was now, inspired by the Pietists, that he preached his first unscripted sermon.

Ever on the lookout for new areas of self-denial to explore, the Methodists decided to go without meat and wine – doubtless with the other passengers' approval – and ate little more than rice and ship's biscuits. ('For what?' demanded their brother Samuel when he heard. Vegetarianism was an 'arrogant and sullen dashing back to God his own grant after the flood'.) Even on this diet, they found themselves wondering if supper was strictly necessary, and soon they went without that too. After a storm, Wesley found his bed soaked and, lying on the floor, slept most soundly. The lesson was clear: 'I believe... I shall not find it needful to go to bed (as it is called) any more.'

They suffered five storms during the voyage and often feared for their lives. Wesley was profoundly disturbed by how little he liked what he saw when he looked death in the face: 'I was unfit, for I was unwilling, to die.' He was ashamed to go to sleep afraid of death and to wake relieved. 'How is it that thou hast no faith?' he demanded. In fact, it seems possible that Wesley suffered from a phobia. He mentioned a few years later his 'fear of the sea, which I had both dreaded and abhorred from my youth' and talked on the journey back about 'unaccountable apprehensions of I knew not what danger'. If so, the condition was to have a serious impact on his spiritual journey.

Wesley recalls one particularly bad storm, which coincided with his attendance at the German passengers' worship:

In the midst of the psalm wherewith their service began, the sea broke over, split the mainsail in pieces, covered the ship, and poured in between the decks, as if the great deep had already swallowed us up. A terrible screaming began among the English. The Germans calmly sung on. I asked one of them afterwards... 'Was you not afraid?'

He answered, 'I thank God, no.'

'But were not your women and children afraid?'

He replied mildly, 'No; our women and children are not afraid to die.'

Who were these steely Germans? The Pietist movement had been started in the 1670s as an attempt by Philipp Jakob Spener to reform the German Lutheran churches by convincing the mass of nominal Christians of the need to be born again and live out a personal faith. Pietists were the first Protestants to take an interest in foreign mission, and it was Susanna's readings about their most notable mission in India that had proved such an attraction when she held services in the rector's absence back in 1712. Some of the group on board were refugees from Salzburg, where 23,000 had been expelled, and were being relocated by Britain so that they could help defend Georgia from attack by Catholic Central America. Others were from the Moravian Brethren, a more radical strand of Pietism led by Count Zinzendorf and based in a commune in Saxony called Herrnhut – they came not as exiles but as missionaries. Wesley was impressed not only by their faith but also by their humility as they performed 'those servile offices for the other passengers, which none of the English would undertake; for which they desired, and would receive no pay, saying, "it was good for their proud hearts"'.

There were many other differences between Moravian religion and Wesley's English kind. They had a strong hymn-singing tradition, more emotional than the English. They put far more emphasis on experience and feelings in the spiritual life and were keen on extempore prayer and preaching. Above all, there was the emphasis on justification by faith that the English Church had lost. Moravian spirituality was to have an incalculable impact on the shape of Methodism.

The journey to Georgia was important for another reason: this was when Wesley's *Journal* started. From their embarkation in Gravesend on 14 October 1735 through to 24 October 1790, Wesley narrated his daily activities and then published them every year or two in a total of 21 instalments. These are not the bare and barren hourly audits of his earlier diary (though he still continued that), but the story of his mission, his trials and triumphs, written to be read.

Such a long and detailed record is invaluable for those interested in Wesley's life and work, but something of a mixed blessing. It is a vast source of information, recording thousands of incidents that would otherwise have sunk into oblivion, and gives an insight into the first

60 years of the Methodist movement from the point of view of a man who was at its heart. The journals of his brother Charles and George Whitefield bear no comparison in their scope or usefulness. Wesley's is highly readable, written with economy, simplicity, drama and sometimes a nice touch of irony – though more often just plain sarcasm.

Yet the lack of other accounts makes it hard to test the reliability of the *Journal*. For one thing, each instalment was written up a matter of years after the events it describes. The journal for Georgia, for example, covering the period from 1735 to the start of 1738, was published in 1740. This is not necessarily a grave problem, as this volume at least was based on fulsome diary entries, and later ones were often based on day-by-day reports that he sent by letter to friends. A greater difficulty is the bias that a discerning reader has to suspect in his accounts. Of course, objectivity is only ever an ideal in any writing, let alone an autobiography, but for Wesley it was not even an ideal. He was not a liar, but he had no scruples about spinning a story for the good of the cause. The *Journal* was written to defend his reputation and broadcast propaganda for Methodism, the first volume being published specifically in an attempt to clear his name from the scandal that followed him home from Georgia. Wesley had a powerful sense of his own rightness, and the *Journal* almost always presents him in a far better light than it does his opponents.

His attitude to other writings provides a hint of his approach to the *Journal*. For example, he castigated Xenophon's *Memorable Things of Socrates* for an amazing want of judgment in including much that showed Socrates in a poor light and objected to certain books of Church history for similar reasons. Thus we can see that Wesley made no distinction between biography and hagiography, and this fact is reflected in his autobiography. In his later work as an editor, whether of classic Christian texts or new writings and hymns, he would, without warning, alter or omit anything that offended his own taste or theology. It would not be surprising if his memories in the *Journal* contained similar subtle revisions of what was said.

There is also the question of what Wesley left out. The *Journal* is basically the chronicle of his work, not of his life. For example, his greatest love affair with Grace Murray, despite being a terrible personal crisis, is never even mentioned, and Grace herself only earns an entry

47

for her conversion nine years earlier. Even his wedding does not warrant a mention. Readers have also often noticed a curious lack of emotional engagement with what he does include. It has been called 'one of the most impersonal documents ever written'. This in itself reveals something about Wesley – his emotional restraint and reserve and his sense of what did and did not deserve to be made public. Of course, it is the case that gushing was not to the taste of 18th-century readers. However, one still wonders what drove Wesley to pour so much of his life into his *Journal* and yet also hold so much back.

The *Simmonds* arrived safely. With the ship still moored on an offshore island, General Oglethorpe went ashore and returned with the leader of the Moravians in America, August Spangenberg, with whom Wesley had a momentous conversation. Voicing his esteem for the Pietists, he asked Spangenberg for advice about his conduct, but the German had more important issues to discuss.

'My brother,' he said, 'I must first ask you one or two questions. Have you the witness within yourself? Does the Spirit of God bear witness with your spirit that you are a child of God?'

Wesley was quite thrown and did not know what to say. Spangenberg pushed him further. 'Do you know Jesus Christ?'

There was a pause. 'I know he is the Saviour of the world,' replied Wesley.

'True; but do you know he has saved you?'

'I hope he has died to save me.'

'Do you know yourself?' urged Spangenberg.

'I do,' Wesley said. 'But', he added afterwards in his *Journal*, 'I fear they were vain words.'[*]

For years, Wesley had been taking his salvation ever more seriously. The more serious he got, the more strenuous his efforts became, but then the more aware he was of how short they fell of his own standards. The idea that certainty of salvation was possible – let alone essential to being saved – was completely alien. In time, this idea

---

[*] Spangenberg's interpretation of the encounter was markedly different: 'I observe that grace really dwells and reigns in him.' Already, the *Journal*'s evidence is proving problematic.

would break him free from his religion of insatiable anxiety. For now, it was just another thing to worry about.

In his early days in Georgia, before his house had been built, he lodged with the Germans, and closer inspection of their Christian life did not disappoint. Wesley eulogized about their way of living, their cheerful good humour, the absence of strife or bitterness, but top of the list was that 'they were always employed'. He witnessed the Moravian ordination of a new bishop and was again bowled over: 'The great simplicity, as well as solemnity, of the whole, almost made me forget the seventeen hundred years between, and imagine myself in one of those assemblies where form and state were not; but Paul the tent-maker, or Peter the fisherman, presided.' It seemed he had found in the Moravians not only holiness and the conquest of idle pleasures, but even primitive Christianity.

In March, John started work as minister of Savannah while Charles went as a stopgap to Georgia's second town, Frederica. The colony as a whole numbered about 500 people. Some were gentry, some debtors who had been allowed to come from English prisons to make a fresh start, some were foreign refugees and some were English Dissenters in search of greater freedom.

John's ministry went down well at first. Admittedly, his confiscation and destruction of the rum brought to celebrate their safe arrival was not well received, but the many who heard his preaching seemed deeply attentive and responsive. Where was the persecution that had always attended his previous efforts? 'We can't see any cloud gathering. But this calm cannot last; storms must come hither too. And let them come.' Whether in pursuit of this end or not, he made it his policy to allow Communion only to those who came to his 5 a.m. service every day of the year. This was widely resented, but Wesley was not equipped to take such criticism on board. He and Delamotte now saw that there was room for further cuts in their diet and decided to live by bread alone, 'to try whether life might not as well be sustained by one sort as by variety of food'.

Charles, meanwhile, was having a miserable time in Frederica. Oglethorpe found him a useless secretary, and the people an insufferable priest. The religious demands he made on them were pedantic, burdensome and unrealistic for frontier life, his enquiries and investigation into their private lives being particularly offensive. He apparently had one Mr Hawkins locked up for hunting for food during public worship.

Then real trouble started. By Charles's account, Mrs Hawkins and her friend Mrs Welch confessed to him that they had fornicated with Governor Oglethorpe. Charles took the allegation seriously, only to find that they complained to Oglethorpe that Charles was spreading these unfounded rumours about them. It then emerged that Charles had been visiting Welch at night – for spiritual exhortation he explained, but she told Oglethorpe another story. Charles and his services were shunned and he was even shot at.

In April 1736, John paid him a visit, a long journey by barge in which he once woke to find himself completely under water, still wrapped from head to foot in the large cloak he used to keep off the flies. He found Charles ill and depressed. John started an investigation – for which Oglethorpe, in the middle of organizing forces to repel a Spanish attack, had little patience. The women baffled Wesley by swinging from tearful shame to violent outrage and from spiritual responsiveness to cold hostility.

In July, Charles resigned the post, leaving on good terms with Oglethorpe who was happy to make the far more efficient John his secretary and advised Charles to take a wife. Returning to England, Charles wrote to John, putting the blame squarely on Hawkins and Welch. The women found out the contents of the letter, which John further explained to them. Welch treated him to the most scurrilous and profane outburst he had ever heard and Hawkins demanded a home visit. He found her in her bedroom where she attacked him with a pair of scissors and a pistol, threatening either to have his heart's blood or cut his hair. While her husband held back the constable and neighbours, Wesley held her by the wrists and she tore into his cassock with her teeth until Mr Hawkins pulled her off.

John was decidedly dividing opinion in Georgia. He had enough of a following to gather the keenest into groups for weekly study and discussion – a pattern inspired by the Moravians that was to be the backbone of Methodism proper, although it was no great success here. Less favourable opinion was represented by a parishioner who told him:

I like nothing you do. All your sermons are satires upon particular persons, therefore I will never hear you more; and all the people are of my mind, for we won't hear ourselves abused. Beside, they say, they are Protestants. But as for you, they cannot tell what religion you are of... All the quarrels that have been here since you came, have been 'long of you. Indeed, there is neither man nor woman in the town who abides a word you say. And so you may preach long enough, but nobody will come to hear you.

Wesley longed more than anything to go to evangelize the natives. However, although he met them on their visits to the townships, Oglethorpe insisted that he stick to his duties as parish priest, and Wesley conceded 'there are heathen enough in Savannah'.

While there, he published his (and America's) first hymn book. Half of the hymns were by Isaac Watts, with some by his father and his brother Samuel, and five of his own translations (and bowdlerizations) of Moravian hymns. Charles had not yet started his hymn-writing career.

As if his hope of escaping female distractions in Georgia had not been mocked enough by Hawkins and Welch, in the summer of 1736 love was in the air again for Wesley, carrying in its train the débacle that was to bring his American adventure to an ignominious end. The girl was Sophy Hopkey, a bright, devout 18-year-old who lived with her uncle and aunt – the former, Tom Causton, being the chief magistrate of Savannah. Wesley first met her in March and immediately feared for his vocational celibacy: 'I am in hourly danger,' he told Charles. 'There are two or three women here, young, pretty, God-fearing. Pray that I may know none of them after the flesh.'

Sophy received his pastoral attentions enthusiastically, which encouraged him to give more time to them, reading to her daily from the spiritual classics. However, as the summer went by, he began to suspect that there was more to his motives than mere ministry. Tom Causton evidently spotted this too. He sent her away from home to live in Frederica, where Wesley currently was, telling him that he was keen to get her off his hands and that she was Wesley's for the marrying.

Wesley made no promises. He was not at all sure marriage would be appropriate to his calling, but if it were, who could be a better choice than

Sophy? She was sweet-natured but serious, tidy but not fastidious, wealthy but not worldly. However, she was miserable in Frederica and even their devotional reading and hymn-singing failed to perk up her spirits. She talked of returning to England, but Wesley appealed to her for the sake of their friendship to stay. To Oglethorpe, the solution was obvious: Wesley should take her back to Savannah when he went in October.

'In what boat?' demanded Wesley.

'She can go in none but yours,' answered Oglethorpe, the promoter of clerical matrimony, 'and indeed there is none so proper.' So it was that Wesley and Sophy embarked.

It was a dangerous journey, and not only for Wesley's celibacy. Alone except for a small crew for six days, he had the chance for an intimate observation of her virtues. She faced danger and discomfort cheerfully, she was open and honest and she once more enjoyed devotional reading and theological discussion with him. Was she ready to die? he asked. Absolutely. 'In this world I expect nothing but misery.'

On the fifth night, they slept under a sail on St Katherine's Island with the sailors on the opposite side, but neither could sleep. In the flickering firelight he asked about her former lover.

'I have promised him either to marry him or no one at all,' she answered.

John was seized by an unpremeditated desire and declared, 'Miss Sophy, I should think myself happy if I was to spend my life with you.'

Sophy started to cry. 'I am in every way unhappy. I won't have Tommy; for he is a bad man. And I can have none else. Sir, you don't know what danger you are in. I beg you to speak no word more on this head.'

A more resolute lover might have leapt the hurdle in a gallant instant, but Wesley lapsed into silence. What he had said could not be unsaid, however: he had not officially proposed, but he had made his feelings clear. Sophy's refusal was, one might have thought, equally transparent, but not to Wesley. Maybe fearing this, she added, 'When others have spoke to me on this subject, I felt an aversion to them. But I don't feel any to you.' They sang a psalm and slept on it.

The following night, Sophy raised the subject of how miserable she would be having to live with her aunt and uncle again. John suggested she could live with the Moravians instead. 'She made little reply.' He watched with admiration as she hung out her apron to keep off the wind, and lay down.

Back in Savannah, Sophy continued to shine as his star disciple and often stayed for breakfast with him and Delamotte after morning prayer. This irritated Delamotte and did nothing to disabuse the public of the impression that they were fast becoming an item. Causton continued to encourage him. About his work as a whole, he felt positive enough to write to the Methodists at home, with a stirring call to any who would come and join the great and glorious labour. It worked on Whitefield, whose heart leapt as he read this, and he decided to come as soon as he could arrange it.

In January 1737, Wesley returned to Frederica, his dietary regime now relaxed enough to allow him to eat boiled bear on the way. However, he had become so unpopular among the flock there as to have his life threatened, persuading him to give the township up as a lost cause.

In Savannah again, he 'groaned under the weight of an unholy desire'. He made another half-hearted proposal attempt that Sophy likewise lacked the heart to close with. If she had, 'my judgment would have made but faint resistance', he reflected.

He asked advice of the Moravian pastor, and John's confused astonishment at the enthusiastic go ahead he gave him suggests what the real point of the exercise was. His Holy Club friends were more forthcoming in their warnings. He spent a week alone in prayer seeking God's will, which was revealed to be the same as Ingham's and Delamotte's: he was not to marry. Miss Sophy had refused, he was not strong enough for the 'temptations of a married state' and it would frustrate his plans to convert the natives.

Yet when he came to explain himself to Miss Sophy, it came out as a somewhat weaker resolution 'not to do so till I have been among the Indians'. It was enough though to make her put on the pressure. She told him she would come no more for breakfast and have no more French lessons from him. When John took this at face value, she was immediately fearful of the tactic and added, 'I will be glad of your coming to our house as often as you please.'

So he visited, and found Sophy in a sharp temper. When he mentioned that he – who had persuaded her to stay in Georgia for 'friendship's sake' – was thinking of returning to England, she was horror-struck. Another time, he was overcome enough to touch her hand. She warmed to his advance and Wesley decided to make a solid proposal there and then – but remembering her resolution not to marry, he changed his mind.

Delamotte and Ingham feared that he would soon be lost to them. Delamotte, in tears, vowed he could not live under the same roof as Mrs Wesley. The three men, following the Moravians' example, decided to discern the mind of God in the biblical way and draw lots. After long prayer, they wrote on three slips of paper 'Marry', 'Think of it not this year' and 'Think of it no more.' For some slightly suspicious reason, it was Delamotte rather than Wesley who drew, and he selected 'Think of it no more.' A second such oracle indicated that John should see Sophy only in the presence of Delamotte. Yet within days, he found himself in her garden, she holding his hand and melting his heart. This time he was only saved by an untimely interruption from Causton.

His dilemma came to a sudden end. Two days later, on 9 March, Mrs Causton asked him to publish the marriage banns between Sophy Hopkey and William Williamson – a man, commented John, 'not remarkable for handsomeness, neither for greatness, or knowledge, or sense, and least of all for religion'. He was utterly distraught. Could he still win Sophy back? Doubtless she herself had half a mind on this outcome and Causton hinted that he could, but even now Wesley vacillated. He opened the Bible at random for guidance (probably another bad idea learned from the Moravians), but failed to make out what God was saying to him. They continued to talk at evening prayer, but when she came home in tears, Williamson demanded a stop to it. Then, on 11 March, Williamson put a stop to it himself by taking her to South Carolina and marrying her there the following day.

From here Wesley's downfall came swiftly. In the early months of her marriage, Sophy's church attendance seemed to dip a little, provoking bitter diatribes from Wesley who demanded full confession of these and more personal failings. In July, she miscarried, which was popularly ascribed to Wesley's abuse.

In August, he barred her from Communion. Biographers have debated whether Wesley was acting from spite or priestly duty here. The most likely answer seems that he convinced himself that the one was the other, so, while with rigid logic he could justify his actions to himself as strict adherence to the canons of Church discipline, the decision was doubtlessly fuelled by resentment. He was, he said, treating her more strictly than he would others because her lapse proved her earlier piety a wicked pretence – the interpretation of a bitter lover. To the people of Savannah, though, it seemed mere malice. His harsh, High Church regime had always been incomprehensible in this frontier community and now, having played with a girl's feelings, he was punishing her for her marriage.

That week, Wesley was arrested at the demand of magistrate Causton. William Williamson wanted £1,000 damages for his wife's defamation. He was released without bail to come before the grand jury of Savannah on 22 August. The court heard an affidavit signed by Mrs Williamson (which she later withdrew) saying that he had often proposed to her and been rejected. He faced ten charges, nine of which concerned his religious regime. (The only one he conceded involved actually being overly lenient.) The tenth – the only charge he was willing to contest, the others being outside the magistrate's jurisdiction – was 'speaking and writing to Mrs Williamson, against her husband's consent'. The jury was massively packed by Causton, who, according to Wesley, also bribed the jurors from the general store. They found against Wesley, but a respectable minority protested and proceedings adjourned while they consulted the colony's trustees in England.

His congregation dwindled alarmingly and his ministry was largely taken over by a South Carolina Dissenter. He began to consider 'whether the Lord did not call me to return to England'. He announced his planned departure in November, but Causton forbade him to go in view of continuing legal action, demanding bail. Wesley refused to pay, insisting that as they kept postponing the trial they should either get on with it or give him his liberty. The court issued an order forbidding anyone to help him leave. Wesley took evening prayer, shook the dust off his feet, and left Georgia, sailing overnight and then struggling on foot through swamp and woodland to Charlestown. On 22 December, he took his leave of America.

CHAPTER 8

LIBERATION
(1738)

'My Chains fell off, my Heart was free.'
From 'And can it be'

Wesley's voyage back to England was a miserable one. For a start, he was seasick and spent Christmas in bed. He had plenty of time to reflect on what had come of his mission to Georgia. His longing to convert the Indians had come to no more than a couple of conversations. His dream of a holy community recapturing the life of the early Church had turned into a nightmare. His insistence on the strictest religious and moral standards had ended in his flying at night from the law. For all his mountainous self-belief and welcoming of persecution, he could not entirely escape the knowledge that his great work had failed and if he had not wavered so long between two opinions about marriage the disaster would not have happened.

The adventure had seriously undermined his spiritual condition. For once, he found it hard to talk to shipmates about religion. He felt fear or sorrow without knowing why. He eventually overcame his diffidence by an effort of the will and this seemed to ease his depression. A return to his ascetic diet seemed to relieve the seasickness.

One healthy outcome of all this was that he saw the fallacy of his long pursuit of holiness in solitude. This had been his motivation at Oxford, his reason for spurning Epworth and his goal in coming to

Georgia. After all, his model Jesus had spent his life going from place to place amid the unholy rabble, and now Wesley realized he had got something seriously wrong in not doing the same.

The greatest trauma for Wesley was that life on the ocean wave brought back his fear and questioning more than ever. His lack of assurance in the face of a watery death troubled him to a greater extent after his conversation with Spangenburg. Hence his famous outburst: 'I went to America, to convert the Indians; but oh! who shall convert me?' It was not a failure to live up to his Christian principles that concerned him – his life was exemplary, he knew, in charity and in self-sacrifice. Rather, what plagued him were the terror and doubt he felt in a moment of peril, which seemed to undermine all the rest.

He landed at Deal on 1 February 1738, where the latest minister to take on Georgia was preparing to set sail – George Whitefield. He was somewhat alarmed to hear that the brother he was crossing the ocean to join was just coming ashore. Wesley's reaction to the news was extraordinary. Wondering whether or not it was right for Whitefield to go, in his absence he asked God's will and drew lots on his behalf. The verdict was 'Let him return to London.' Without even speaking to him, he left the instruction in a letter and left town. When Whitefield came ashore for the night, he read the letter, replied with the utmost deference and set sail the following day.

Wesley's state of mind as he returned to England is a puzzle. According to his published *Journal*, he had lost all hope of salvation, realizing that he had been trusting in his own fruitless works and had no faith. He was 'alienated... from the life of God', '"a child of wrath", an heir of hell'. This account, however, was written after his evangelical conversion and is highly coloured by it. His private diary does not go nearly so far, and his letters strongly suggest that he still considered himself and all of the Holy Club to be in a state of grace. Moreover, his outward activity gave the exact opposite impression to that of his *Journal*: he threw himself immediately into itinerant preaching, talking privately and publicly wherever he went about the necessity of faith and spiritual rebirth – so controversially that he was repeatedly asked not to return. This is the precise pattern of his evangelical campaign, months before his experience in Aldersgate Street in May.

The change in his attitude came as a result of his conversations with Peter Böhler, a Moravian missionary heading to Georgia. Meeting him at the house of a mutual acquaintance on 7 February – 'a day much to be remembered' – Wesley found accommodation for him in London and visited him, every chance he had, to discuss theology. It was Böhler who told Wesley that he had no saving faith: he believed intellectually, but still hoped to become righteous by virtue of his own deeds, lacking the true faith that comes in an instant, bringing rebirth and an utter certainty of salvation.

Wesley was confused and uncertain about this, but found Böhler's ideas compelling. He made a typically logical case for his position, but Böhler's response was merely, 'My brother, my brother, that philosophy of yours must be purged away.' Böhler also got to work on Charles in Oxford, and it was there, talking with the two of them, that John finally, on Sunday 5 March, accepted that he lacked saving faith. Naturally he thought he should stop preaching, but Böhler would not hear of it.

'But what can I preach?' asked John.

'Preach faith till you have it; and then, because you have it, you will preach faith.'

An unorthodox answer maybe, but psychologically brilliant, because such preaching is precisely what gradually built up Wesley's faith and confidence in his salvation.

Wesley followed Böhler's advice, meeting the following day with a condemned man in the castle prison. It was the first time, by his own reckoning, that he offered someone salvation by faith alone. It was also the first time that he consented to evangelize someone at the point of death, having until now denied the possibility of instantaneous conversion.

In many ways, this, rather than his Aldersgate experience in May, was Wesley's real evangelical conversion – the acceptance that God can only be appeased by putting faith in his grace, not by attempts at holiness – and by his own account it brought an extraordinary new power to his evangelistic mission. Riding for two weeks from Oxford to Manchester and back, he and his companions talked to every person they met about faith and repentance. Listeners burst into tears and went on their way rejoicing, hostile and indifferent hearts were suddenly melted, while the righteous listened attentively.

The journey also happens to illustrate another couple of Wesley's quirks. One is his superstition: 'The next day we dined at Birmingham; and, soon after we left it, were reproved for our negligence there, in letting those who attended us go without either exhortation or instruction, by a severe shower of hail.' The other is his self-righteousness: 'In the afternoon one overtook us whom we soon found more inclined to speak than to hear.' Without a glimmer of irony, he adds, 'However, we spoke and spared not.' The next morning this fellow 'not only spoke less than the day before but took in good part a serious caution against talkativeness and vanity'.

Back in Oxford, Wesley spent Easter Monday with another condemned man, and was able to give him such assurance of God's forgiveness that he went to his death in perfect peace and confidence. (One of the main demands of life from the Methodist point of view was to die well.) Yet on the Sunday, as he preached on 'The hour cometh, and now is, when the dead shall hear the voice of the son of God, and they that hear shall live,' he said to himself. 'I see the promise, but it is afar off.'

Seeing Peter Böhler again, he was more than ever convinced by the idea of perfect assurance brought by the gift of living faith, but was still questioning how this transformation could be instantaneous. Yet searching through the Bible, he found the book of Acts full of such instant conversions. 'That was then, this is now,' was his only answer to that, but then Böhler introduced him to various people who, like himself, had had the same experience. After this, all Wesley could do was to cry, 'Lord, help thou my unbelief.' He preached Böhler's doctrine to his friends, many of whom, at least at first, were worried by it, and Charles was particularly angered. They thought his talk of having no faith was demonstrably untrue and were offended by its implications for their own faith. 'If you was not a Christian ever since I knew you,' said one angrily, 'you was a great hypocrite.'

On 1 May, they founded another religious group known as the Fetter Lane Society – a successor to the Holy Club and the attempted groups in Georgia, and a predecessor of the Methodist societies proper. Its 11-point constitution claimed the authority of an incongruous pair – 'the command of God by St James' and 'the advice of Peter Böhler'.

They were to meet weekly to confess their sins and pray for healing. They would divide into groups of from five to ten (an optimistic rule as they started out with nine members) and each person was to 'speak as freely, plainly and concisely as he can, the real state of his heart, with his several temptations and deliverances, since the last time of meeting'. The idea of plain speaking was becoming an obsession for the Methodists, and they placed the greatest value on 'being free' with one another and hearing others' opinions of their faults and errors.

John's emotions were in turmoil. At one meeting, his heart was so full of joy that he for once could not confine himself to read prayers and so immediately decided to abandon the practice for life. His heart was equally 'enlarged' in the pulpit, preaching with passionate conviction and being repeatedly told he was not welcome to return. Yet at other times, he suffered protracted sorrow and heaviness.

Charles, meanwhile, had swung from hostility towards Böhler's doctrine to embracing it, and he beat John to claiming the experience himself. Typically, suffering even greater emotional turbulence than his brother, he went down with his second recent bout of pleurisy. (The previous bout had almost killed him.) After John spent the night in prayer for him, Charles heard a voice in his room say, 'In the name of Jesus Christ of Nazareth arise and believe, and thou shalt be healed of all thy infirmities.' He thought it might have been the voice of Christ, but it turned out to be one Mrs Musgrave who had come to see him after being given the words in a dream. He was indeed relieved of his pleurisy and wondered if he had been given the perfect assurance of salvation he sought. The fact that he had to ask a friend suggests not. All that day he prayed and struggled until, finally, 'I found myself at peace with God, and rejoiced in the hope of loving Christ... I saw that by faith I stood; and the continual support of faith which kept me from falling.' Two days later, he embarked on his career as a hymn-writer with a hymn about his conversion – variously supposed to be either 'Where shall my wandering soul begin?' or 'And can it be?' – though he nearly abandoned it halfway through for fear of his pride in it.

John's response to this was to plunge into three days of despondency. On the third day, Wednesday 24 May, he opened his Bible on the words 'Thou art not far from the kingdom of God' and felt himself bombarded by similar messages throughout the day. In the evening, he forced himself to go to the famous meeting off Aldersgate Street, where one of the largely Moravian society was reading from Luther's *Preface to Romans*:

> About a quarter before nine, while he was describing the change which God works in the heart through faith in Christ, I felt my heart strangely warmed. I felt I did trust in Christ, Christ alone, for salvation; and an assurance was given me that He had taken away my sins, even mine, and saved me from the law of sin and death.

This, then, is Wesley's famous 'conversion' – the most celebrated in the history of the English-speaking world. However, if it was a conversion, then to what? Not Christianity per se of course, as he had always believed it, and not from nominal Christianity to the real thing, as few Christians alive in the 1730s could have been less nominal than Wesley. Conversion to evangelical Christianity would be getting warmer, but as we have seen, Wesley already accepted all the evangelical teachings of the Moravians before this particular day. It was clearly a powerful spiritual experience and John interpreted it as the gift of faith – the moment when in both heart and head he finally reached confidence in his salvation. Yet the fact is that this confidence, as we shall see, was very short-lived, which seriously undermines the significance of the experience. It is possible to see this supposed receipt of the gift of assurance as the emotional culmination of his turning from a pursuit of salvation through the rigours of self-sanctification, to salvation by faith alone through his mere trust in Christ's own achievement. However, it seems to have had little long-term importance in Wesley's spiritual journey as genuine assurance actually came to him through a much steeper climb, and so little if anything had genuinely changed. Also, before long, he would vehemently reject much of what the Moravians had told him about faith. Aldersgate Street was just another turning in the road, but for the moment he felt he had come home.

Wesley's spirit had apparently found peace, yet he was immediately troubled that this did not make him feel happier, which in turn undermined his confidence in his faith, though he pushed such doubts away. He was also immediately troubled with temptations, but he overcame these too. His success he ascribed to the conquest of all sin that the Moravians had promised would accompany faith. He considered it the chief difference of his new life: yes he was still 'striving, yea, fighting with all my might'; 'but then I was sometimes, if not often, conquered; now, I was always conqueror'.

Over the next two weeks, Wesley was an emotional weathervane, spinning from exultation to anxiety as the wind blew. He put such store on his feelings as proof of his soul's state that the motion of joy when it came would exhilarate him, but as soon as the feeling subsided it was as if God 'hid his face'.

Three weeks after his Aldersgate experience, Wesley left the country. Accompanied once again by Ingham, he went for three months to Herrnhut and other Moravian communities in Germany to visit the home of the movement and its founding leader, Count Zinzendorf, whom he had often written to. His letters to his mother, his brothers and the Fetter Lane Society were full of exuberant praise for the love, piety and candour of the Moravians. 'The spirit of the brethren is beyond our highest expectations,' he told Charles. 'Young and old, they breathe nothing but faith and love, at all times and in all places.' A month after he returned to England, he wrote to the Germans, extravagantly thanking and praising them.

All of which makes it extraordinary that, as soon as he returned to England, he wrote an earlier letter to the Moravians – though he never sent it – full of bitter criticism:

> Do you not wholly neglect joint fasting?
> Is not the Count all in all? Are not the rest mere shadows?...
> Do you not sometimes fall into trifling conversation?
> Do you not magnify your own church too much? Do you believe any who are not of it to be in gospel liberty?
> Are you not straitened in your love?... Do you not use cunning, guile, or dissimulation in many cases?

What was going on? The answer seems to lie in the fourth point above, and in the fact, about which John kept very quiet, that in Marienborn the Moravians allegedly refused him (but not Ingham) Communion. Their reason for this was that his faith was too unsettled and too cerebral and he was too attached to the Church of England. With this insult, the believers he so admired and who had been so instrumental in his own transformation impugned both his salvation and his beloved Church. This left him with very mixed feelings about the Moravians. At the time he wrote the first, unsent letter, his resentment evidently made him uncharitable to any other flaws in their behaviour that he had seen. Wisely, he slept on it, and by the time he wrote later, his admiration for them had regained the ascendancy. The ill feeling was not dead, however, but merely sleeping and would before long rise again to wreak absolute havoc.

CHAPTER 9

THE GOSPEL IN THE FIELDS
(1738–39)

'And publish abroad His wonderful Name'

From 'Ye servants of God, your master proclaim'

Wesley returned to London on 16 September 1738 and, in his own words, 'I began again to declare in my own country the glad tidings of salvation.' This of course is where the story really starts.

For six months, Wesley, along with other Methodist friends including Charles, divided his time between London and Oxford, in one church after another preaching new birth to the masses, taking the message to workhouses and prisons, especially to the condemned, reinvigorating and reorganizing the many religious societies he was connected with (there were about 30 groups in London at the time) and preaching there. The first full day he was in town, he preached four times, and this was not to prove at all unusual. For a wider audience he published his sermons too.

The controversial message often drew large congregations and often offended them, or at least their ecclesiastical overseers. On 5 November, '[I preached] in the evening, to such a congregation as I never saw before, at St Clement's, in the Strand. As this was the first time of my preaching here, I suppose it is to be the last.' This tone of resigned rejection runs right through this phase of his *Journal*. Others, however, responded with all their hearts and Wesley saw 'very many persons changed in a moment from the spirit of horror, fear, and despair, to the spirit of hope, joy, peace'. The violent became gentle, drunkards sober and pimps chaste. To any who disapproved of his ways, these were his 'living arguments'.

However, they were also living arguments for the opposition. People believing themselves suddenly and miraculously changed by divine power presented a worrying new trend and, to make matters worse, the miracle was often worked in a dream or vision. Wesley embraced these phenomena unreservedly, but both his message and these reactions to it rang alarm bells throughout the establishment. You start off with miracles and visions, you end up cutting off the king's head. It was confirmed: Methodists were 'enthusiasts'. [*]

The 1767 satire, *Methodism Triumphant*, illustrates how all this looked to the public. The Methodist narrator summons his muse:

O thou celestial source of ecstasies,
Of visions, raptures and converting dreams...
Thee, Mania, I invoke my pen to guide.

A Plain and Easy Road to the Land of Bliss (1761) has the Methodist dismissing true Anglicans: 'They use their reason to explain things, which is a sure way to be deceived; whereas we go by but puffs, dreams, visions, reveries, voices, etc., etc., all which are the truth itself.'

More scandalous still were the charismatic phenomena that Wesley's preaching started to provoke. Preaching in St Thomas's workhouse, he was interrupted by a young woman crying out from her overwhelming sense of sin, according to one witness, or in John's words 'raving mad, screaming and tormenting herself'. Breaking off his sermon, he came and prayed with her. As he assured her 'Jesus of Nazareth is able and

---

[*] The literal meaning of 'enthusiast' is 'one inspired by God', hence a fanatic who claims divine revelations. Although in Wesley's time, the term was sometimes used almost as vaguely as 'fundamentalist' is in ours – meaning 'one who takes religion more seriously than the present speaker approves of' – it still generally reflected a fear of those who claimed visions and messages from on high. As the Bishop of Bristol, Joseph Butler, told Wesley, 'The pretending to extraordinary revelations and gifts of the Holy Ghost is a horrid thing, a very horrid thing.'

willing to deliver you,' she became quiet, and not only she but many of the congregation were moved to tears.

Such things happened in private too. Wesley got into an argument with a fervent opponent, but as his reasoning only inflamed her further, he stopped and asked to pray with her instead. As they knelt, she was, after a few minutes, racked with violent pain, physical and emotional, which ended with her crying, 'Now I know I am forgiven for Christ's sake.'

Even the Methodist's own inner circle had a taste of charismata, though of a more positive kind. On New Year's Day at Fetter Lane, 60 of them joined for a 'love feast' – consisting of bread and water – including his brother Charles, Ingham, Westley Hall and Whitefield, who had just returned after a year in Georgia. They prayed through the night, until at 3 a.m., Wesley records,

> The power of God came mightily upon us, insomuch that many cried out for exceeding joy, and many fell to the ground. As soon as we were recovered a little from that awe and amazement at the presence of His Majesty, we broke out with one voice, 'We praise Thee, O God; we acknowledge Thee to be the Lord.'

Wesley had still not seen the end of doubts about his spiritual state, however. Once, being reminded that Jesus said, 'The kingdom of God is within you,' he was worried by how little he saw when he looked within himself. The answer to this – as most other questions – was to open the Bible, reading that even Jesus 'also waited for the kingdom of God'. However, if Wesley was to wait, the old question returned of whether or not he should stop his packed preaching schedule. Again his random bibliomancy answered him, 'By works was faith made perfect': preaching would strengthen his faith.

In January 1739, Wesley wrote the last of his spiritual self-audits. If his evangelical conversion was all it was supposed to be, this would surely have rejoiced in his salvation and new life, but nothing could have been further from the truth. He refers back to his experience at Aldersgate Street as a powerful one-off experience of forgiveness, but no more. Since then he had failed to feel the love, joy and peace that true faith inevitably brings, and so he insisted, 'I am not a Christian.'

It was in this state of mind that, in March 1739, Wesley received a life-changing call from George Whitefield.

Whitefield's time in Georgia had been as triumphant as Wesley's had been disastrous. Even before he went, he had turned out to be a phenomenally popular preacher in London and Bristol, preaching nine times a week in church, and twice as often to the societies. As Whitefield recorded in his *Journal*:

> On Sunday mornings, long before day, you see streets filled with people going to church, with their lanthorns [lanterns] in their hands, and hear them conversing about the things of God. Other lecture Churches near at hand would be filled with persons who could not come where I was preaching; and those who did come were like persons struck with pointed arrows or mourning for a firstborn child...
>
> In a short time I could no longer walk on foot as usual, but was constrained to go in a coach, from place to place, to avoid the hosannas of the multitude.

While waiting to sail in Deal, he took to dividing the congregation into two sittings so that both could hear him. Even then the floor of the hall had to be strengthened to bear their weight.

In Georgia, his gospel proved far more favourable than Wesley's had been. He left, hoping to return before long, saying, 'The longer I continued there, the larger the congregations grew. And I scarce knew a night, though we had Divine service twice a day, when the Church House has not been nearly full.'

He had spent the first two months since his return from Georgia preaching in London, praying for his opponents, moving the societies to tears with his words and taking a collection for an orphanage in Georgia. He had moved on to Bristol in February and there his mission took off more spectacularly than ever. Turned away from most churches – both for his evangelical theology and his histrionic homiletics – and threatened by the Chancellor with excommunication, he preached at the societies to so many hundreds that the stairs and courts below were crammed with latecomers straining to hear.

Then one Saturday, he visited the mining community of Kingswood, an underclass with the worst living conditions in Britain, abhorred by locals as animals and beyond the pale of the established Church. Shunned by the churches himself, Whitefield was reminded of something he had contemplated in London when an overflow of a thousand had filled the churchyard and hundreds more had turned home: outdoor preaching. His friends had told him it was insane. It was certainly the Methodists' most disreputable move yet, bringing still more unwelcome echoes of the Puritan revolution. However, that afternoon, after taking dinner, Whitefield recalled, 'I went upon a mount, and spake to as many people as came unto me. They were upwards of two hundred. Blessed be God, I have now broken the ice!'

The echo of that other well-known sermon on a mount is, one suspects, not accidental.

By the time he wrote to Wesley, Whitefield was preaching – outdoors and in – to thousands. One sunny day at Kingswood, 10,000 turned up, filling the trees and bushes in their efforts to hear. Elsewhere, he once purportedly attracted 23,000.[*]

Whitefield also used his eloquence to raise great sums to found a local charity school for the miners' children. He had become the brightest light of the Methodist gospel and now he was off on a preaching and fund-raising tour. He half-implored, half-summoned Wesley to come and take over, suggesting it was time to start organizing the converts into 'bands' – small, regular spiritual support groups. This was indeed Wesley's forte rather than Whitefield's, but it was not as if he was short of an audience in London, and the Fetter Lane Society were not at all sure about releasing John from his thriving work. Charles especially would not hear of losing him – until, that is, he opened the Bible on the words 'Son of Man, behold, I take from thee

---

[*] It should be borne in mind that the sizes of gatherings given in the Methodist revival are doubtful. I have quoted numbers throughout from the preachers' own accounts, which are almost the only sources available, but some exaggeration seems likely. No more accurate estimates are obtainable, and of course, even after making allowances for hyperbole, the numbers are remarkable.

the desire of thine eyes with a stroke,' and that seemed to settle the matter. A little lot-drawing and much communal text-chopping followed. (The precise implication of 'And Ahab slept with his fathers and they buried him in the city, even in Jerusalem' is not immediately obvious, but apparently indicated that death awaited Wesley in Bristol and, therefore, that he should go.)

Finally it was agreed and Wesley arrived in Bristol on Saturday 31 March 1739. He was shocked on the Sunday morning to witness Whitefield preaching on a bowling green – 'having been all my life (till very lately)', stressed Wesley, 'so tenacious of every point relating to order, that I should have thought the saving of souls almost a sin if it were not done in church'. His recent experiences had been mellowing him, but this was still a hard pill to swallow.

The next day, Whitefield left, with John praying for 'some portion of his spirit', but rather than follow his example into the fields, Wesley preached at one of the local societies to a packed and overflowing hall. His choice of text was significant, though: the Sermon on the Mount – 'One pretty remarkable precedent of field-preaching,' he reflected. The day after, Monday 2 April, he went to one of Whitefield's pulpits, a mound in a brickyard, and took the plunge:

> At four in the afternoon, I submitted to be more vile, and
> proclaimed in the highways the glad tidings of salvation, speaking
> from a little eminence in a ground adjoining the city, to about
> three thousand people.

Again the text is not without a sense of occasion:

> The Spirit of the Lord is upon me, because He hath anointed
> me to preach the gospel to the poor. He hath sent me to heal
> the broken-hearted; to preach deliverance to the captives, and
> recovery of sight to the blind; to set at liberty the bruised, to
> proclaim the acceptable year of the Lord (Luke 4:18–19).

The crowds took to him immediately as the new Whitefield and it was not long before he was regularly drawing crowds of up to 5,000, by his reckoning. Whitefield seems to have been the more compelling preacher, certainly the more dramatic. Both Wesley and Whitefield were accused by Horace Walpole of being actors, but it was of the latter that the actor David Garrick said, 'I'd give a hundred guineas if I could say "Oh!" like Mr Whitefield,' adding that he could bring an audience to tears with his delivery of the word 'Mesopotamia'. One of his tricks was, towards the end of a sermon, suddenly to stop, and raise his hand. 'The attendant angel is about to leave the threshold of this sanctuary and ascend to heaven,' he would announce. Then he would stamp, and raise his eyes. 'Stop, Gabriel! Stop! And carry with you the news of yet one more sinner converted to God.' 'We scarce know what it is', Whitefield once told a Baptist minister, 'to have a meeting without tears.' Dr Johnson, who thought well of Wesley, said that Whitefield attracted crowds merely by 'familiarity and noise' and would have the same effect 'were he to wear a night-cap in the pulpit, or were he to preach from a tree'.

Wesley did not, gifted speaker though he was, have the same rhetorical flamboyance as Whitefield. Wesley's first biographer, his somewhat embittered former lay preacher John Hampson, said that 'his style was the calm, equal flow of a placid stream'. He was convincing, but 'never soared into sublimity', while Whitefield was a master of others' emotions.

Wesley's gift was rather for presenting a logical theological case in a way that could be easily followed and accepted by ordinary listeners. If that sounds a little dull, he had something else less easy to put one's finger on – a powerful charismatic presence. John Nelson, later to be one of his first lay preachers, described its effect on him the first time he saw him:

> As soon as he got upon the stand, he stroked back his hair, and turned his face towards where I stood, and I thought fixed his eyes upon me. His countenance struck such an awful dread upon me, before I heard him speak, that it made my heart beat like the pendulum of a clock; and, when he did speak, I thought his whole discourse was aimed at me.

One Elizabeth Hinton said, 'He told me my heart... And when I looked at him I thought he spake to me only.' Hampson thought his eyes 'the brightest and most piercing that can be conceived'. 'Few have seen him,' he continued, 'without being struck by his appearance; and many, who had been greatly prejudiced against him, have been known to change their opinion the moment they were introduced to his presence.' This may sound like sycophantic fancy, but Hampson was not a sycophant, and there is ample evidence for what he said.

Wesley had another crowd-pulling sensation at hand too – the supernatural. As in London, these phenomena started in the religious societies. On 17 April at the Baldwin Street meeting, one woman started crying out 'as if in the agonies of death'. She was prayed for and ended up rejoicing. Then, several other people – well known, Wesley was at pains to point out, for their good lives – started roaring 'as out of the belly of hell'. In each case the horrors soon subsided into the joy of knowing that they were accepted by God.

Once it had begun, this kind of thing happened almost daily. What brought it to a wider public was, oddly enough, a debate over predestination. This was a subject on which Wesley and Whitefield were at odds. Whitefield was a passionately committed predestinarian.[*] Wesley was an equally passionate believer in free will – but they had agreed to let sleeping dogmas lie. What divided them, was for now, less important than the message that united them. However, the fact that their Fetter Lane friends – Whitefield himself and others – repeatedly warned Wesley of the dangers of stirring up the controversy suggests an anxiety about his propensity to go to war over theological molehills and, if so, they were quite right. On 24 April, he received a letter, already widely circulated, berating him for perverting the gospel by his denial of predestination. The challenge was irresistible.

On 26 April, he was preaching at Newgate Gaol (a favourite haunt that was open to all comers), when, without any previous design, he said, he found himself inwardly called to speak out vehemently against predestination. After making the point at length, he prayed aloud (again on divine impulse) that if he was right, God would send a sign. Wesley records:

---

* The doctrines at issue were that only those chosen by God can be saved, that the elect cannot lose their salvation, and that Christ died only for the elect.

Immediately the power of God fell upon us. One, and another, and another, sunk to the earth. You might see them, dropping on all sides as thunderstruck. One cried out aloud. I went and prayed over her, and she received joy in the Holy Ghost. A second falling into the same agony, we turned to her, and received for her also the promise of the Father.

Wesley's preaching was becoming a noisy event, which of course only further outraged his many opponents, as well as closing doors that had been open to him until now. Wesley tells of a local doctor who denounced the antics of his smitten hearers as fraud, only to see a female patient he had known for many years weeping, wailing, sweating and shaking. 'When both her body and soul were healed in an instant, he acknowledged the finger of God.' Another angry spectator, a Quaker, was making disapproving faces when he himself keeled over in agony. 'We besought God not to lay folly to his charge. And he soon lifted up his head, and cried aloud, "Now I know thou art a prophet of the Lord."'

John did not even have to be present himself to have this effect. John Haydon, a devout churchman and a weaver, came to see the performance at Baldwin Street and went round all his friends afterwards warning them that it was the work of the Devil. He went home and read Wesley's published sermon *Salvation by Faith*. In the final rousing paragraph, 'he changed colour, fell off his chair and began screaming and beating himself against the ground'. Neighbours crowded in to watch and tried to hold him down. When Mrs Haydon tried to keep spectators out, he cried, 'No let them all come, let all the world see the just judgment of God.' In the early hours, Wesley was brought over. Seeing him, Haydon called out to the demons that they would be cast out and, sure enough, Wesley's prayers brought him peace.

The genuinely involuntary nature of at least some of these occurrences is suggested by, for example, the report of a woman who felt a profound sense of her sinfulness coming over her in a meeting and ran out of the building to avoid making a spectacle of herself. She collapsed outside and was carried home, where Wesley found her in pain and brought her relief.

What is one to make of these charismatic phenomena? They happened to men and women, though significantly more to the latter it seems, to children as young as 10 and mostly the lower classes, as that is primarily the grouping his audiences consisted of. The image of Wesley wading through the fallen as in a battlefield, praying over the shaking, hyperventilating bodies, will sound oddly familiar to any who witnessed the 'Toronto blessing' in 1994. Wesley's account was profoundly shaped by the needs of PR: he was trying to justify himself to a sceptical readership, showing that these scandalous occurrences were quite involuntary, happening to the most upright and rational people, sceptics even, with the most positive results for their spiritual lives, and therefore should be seen as stamping Divine approval on Wesley's work rather than discrediting it. Also, he insisted, they were quite unlike the epileptic and hysterical fits he had often seen. Nevertheless, even Wesley's interpretation of the phenomena does not appear to have been entirely straightforward and he refused to be dogmatic about it – a certain sign that he was not sure what to think. However, piecing together the impressions given in his reports, a fairly consistent picture emerges. He saw the screams of pain and horror as the result of revelations of hell given to complement his warnings about the end of the unrepentant and/or expressing grief for one's sin, but also as the last stand of the evil spirit that inhabits all unbelievers and is unhappy about the prospect of being dispossessed. Joy came with the assurance from God that one had been delivered from the infernal torments witnessed and with the expulsion of the Devil by the Holy Spirit. Seen like this, the popular question of whether or not the episode was from the hand of God or of Satan did not really apply: it was the result of their mutual conflict. At other times, though, especially in private, he was happy to say simply 'the power of God fell mightily among us'. In a letter written a number of years later, he talked of the fits in terms of the Spirit 'sharply convincing the soul of sin'. Whichever way one looked at it, the outcome was God's and its reflection on Wesley's ministry was wholly positive.

Wesley's contemporaries, including some fellow Methodists, were more sceptical. Modern readers will have such scepticism amplified by a century of psychologizing and secularism, but maybe also somewhat muted by the last century's accommodation of charismatic experience into mainstream Christian life. It would be presumptuous to attempt to psychoanalyse Wesley's audience at this distance, but a few observations can usefully be made. Hearers at the religious societies were in their thousands and crammed into halls filled well beyond their capacity, often early in the morning or late at night – ideal conditions for a speaker who wants to have a devastating emotional impact. Conditions at Newgate must have been similar. Moreover, Wesley was, despite his relatively short stature, a man of extraordinarily compelling presence, and he could draw a powerful emotional response. We must also remember that the everlasting physical torture of damnation and the need to be saved from it were utterly solid realities for ordinary people of the time. Consequently, the Methodist message – that no one was saved until he or she was born again – was, for those who took it seriously, one provoking real terror. Jonathan Edwards's notorious sermon *Sinners in the Hand of an Angry God* (which reduced a whole congregation in Enfield, Connecticut, to loud throes of desolate anguish with its depiction of a disgusted God keeping them for the moment out of a nightmarish eternal holocaust on a mere whim) was only a distillation of the same essence.

CHAPTER 10

THE OFFENCE OF THE GOSPEL (1739)

'Poor Outcasts of Men'

From 'Let all men rejoice, by Jesus restored'

After just a month in Bristol, Wesley was able to obtain a piece of land in the Horse Fair, where they began building the New Room – the first purpose-built Methodist meeting hall. It was to be a place for indoor preaching, for the societies that had been meeting in Baldwin Street and Nicholas Street and a school for local children. The money for it was supposed to be raised by society members, overseen by a board of trustees, but this was not working, so Wesley himself had to borrow the money. Persuaded, quite easily and quite rightly, of the dangers of being a preacher at the mercy of his landlords, he sacked the trustees and took sole oversight. Wesley's biographer Martin Schmidt convincingly pinpoints this as a crucial moment when Wesley gained his independence, becoming a Methodist leader in his own authority, instead of working as he always had done in consultation with his peers. It also fortuitously put him in a position of strength in the times of conflict that lay ahead. Wesley organized the converts there into bands of from five to ten members with a leader, yet another process that was decided by lot.

As Wesley's audiences grew, opposition increased. Henry Stebbing, a royal chaplain, had an anti-Methodist bestseller with *A Caution against Religious Delusion*, which went through six editions in as many months.

One Monday in May, as Wesley was setting out to preach in Pensford church, he was given a note: 'Sir, our minister, having been informed you are beside yourself, does not care that you should preach in any of his churches.' He went anyway and preached on a nearby common.

On one of his frequent trips to Bath, he was warned by friends not to preach because Beau Nash, the most prominent figure in fashionable society, was planning to confront him. This made no difference at all to Wesley, except that it increased his audience, bringing out many of the wealthy classes who had rarely paid him any attention before. He took the chance to pick on them, telling them that rich and poor alike were in equal danger of God's judgment, but just as he felt he was getting through, Nash turned up and demanded to know by what authority Wesley was acting in this way:

I replied, 'By the authority of Jesus Christ, conveyed to me by the (now) Archbishop of Canterbury, when he laid hands upon me and said, "Take thou authority to preach the gospel."'

He said, 'This is contrary to the Act of Parliament: this is a conventicle.'

I answered, 'Sir, the conventicles mentioned in that Act (as the preamble shows) are seditious meetings; but this is not such; here is no shadow of sedition; therefore it is not contrary to that Act.'

He replied, 'I say it is: and beside, your preaching frightens people out of their wits.'

'Sir, did you ever hear me preach?'

'No.'

'How, then, can you judge of what you never heard?'

'Sir, by common report.'

'Common report is not enough. Give me leave, Sir, to ask, is not your name Nash?'

'My name is Nash.'

'Sir, I dare not judge of you by common report: I think it not enough to judge by.'

Here he paused awhile and, having recovered himself, said, 'I desire to know what this people comes here for': on which one replied, 'Sir, leave him to me: let an old woman answer him. You,

Mr Nash, take care of your body; we take care of our souls; and
for the food of our souls we come here.' He replied not a word,
but walked away.

The streets afterwards were full of commotion, and people were asking
each other 'Which one is Wesley?' Several wealthy women finding him
at a local house told the maid they wished to speak with him. He came
out to them, saying, 'I believe, ladies, the maid mistook: you wanted
only to look at me.'

The same week, two singers were paid to interrupt his sermon by
performing a ballad. Reasoning with them failed, so the faithful
congregation started singing a psalm themselves, which silenced the
singers. 'We then poured out our souls in prayer for them, and they
appeared altogether confounded.'

It was not just fear of disorder that made alfresco sermons
controversial. It also offended parish priests and their sympathizers
because wherever Wesley preached he was in someone's parish,
invading his pastures and worrying his sheep. It was in defence from
such accusations, rather than as a general statement of vocation, that
he made the famous declaration that the world was his parish:

God in Scripture commands me, according to my power, to
instruct the ignorant, reform the wicked, confirm the virtuous.
Man forbids me to do this in another's parish; that is, in effect, to
do it at all, seeing I have now no parish of my own, nor probably
ever shall. Whom then shall I hear, God or man?...

I look upon *all the world* as *my parish*; thus far I mean, that,
in whatever part of it I am, I judge it meet, right, and my bounden
duty to declare unto all that are willing to hear, the glad tidings
of salvation. This is the work which I know God has called me to;
and sure I am that his blessing attends it.

'Nor can I be said,' he added on another occasion, in answer to
Stebbing's animadversion, 'to "intrude into the labours" of those who
do not labour at all, but suffer thousands of those for whom Christ died
to "perish for lack of knowledge".'

Wesley remained utterly loyal to the Church of England, for all his troublemaking. Nevertheless, his hardline dismissal of the Dissenters was thawing. He prayed with Quakers, and 'our hearts were much enlarged one to another'. When a Dissenting woman applied to join the bands he was organizing, he warmed to the idea, on account of her holiness and deep experience. Opening the Bible for an oracle on the question, his impulse was confirmed by a text about the heathen being justified by faith; but he cast lots anyway and was instructed to refer the matter to Fetter Lane.

If this superstition allowed him to create new friendships, it also allowed him to destroy invaluable older ones. What should he do about the predestination question that was causing friction between him and others such as Whitefield? Continue to declare 'the whole counsel of God' or let it rest? Print the controversial sermon he had preached on it* or leave it in the oral tradition? Whitefield begged him neither to print nor preach, as did many friends of his own opinion, and something within him concurred. However, others urged him not to compromise the truth and something within him concurred with that too. So, once again, he resorted to pulling God's will out of a hat and was told 'Print and preach', which he did.

It was an extremely powerful piece of writing, a violent excoriation of 'the blasphemy clearly contained in the horrible decree of predestination'. It destroys our comfort, holiness and zeal for preaching, he insisted, or if it does not, it logically should do. 'It represents the most holy God as worse than the Devil, as both more false, more cruel, and more unjust.' It is clearly taught in the Bible, its defenders say. Nonsense, says Wesley, skating briskly over thin ice, it is a monstrous doctrine and therefore cannot possibly be biblical. It was a sermon to fortify those who already agreed with him, not one to win round the opposition – rather, it fortified them too. This is the fault line that was to tear the evangelical movement in two.

Wesley had to return to London for a week in June to see to various disputes and conflicts at Fetter Lane. He was able to reconcile them

---

* This is not his impromptu sermon of 26 April 1739 (see pp. 71–72), but a more considered exposition probably preached three days later.

and led them in repentance for their faithlessness. 'In that hour, we found God with us as at the first. Some fell prostrate upon the ground. Others burst out, as with one consent, into loud praise and thanksgiving.'

More dramatic outbursts occurred when he visited a society in Wapping. He preached on a text that came into his head at the last moment and drew tears and roars from the crowd. As Wesley recorded in his *Journal*:

> Some sunk down, and there remained no strength in them; others exceedingly trembled and quaked; some were torn with a kind of convulsive motion in every part of their bodies, and that so violently that four or five persons could not hold one of them... One woman was greatly offended, being sure they might help it if they would – no one should persuade her to the contrary; and was got three or four yards, when she also dropped down in as violent agony as the rest.

Continuing his enquiry into the nature and meaning of these strange things, he asked 26 of those affected to report back to him the following day. Of these, 18 turned up and some of them he was convinced had genuinely found forgiveness from God. The rest were patiently waiting for it.

He met with his mother while in London. She was alarmed by what she had been hearing about him. A relative had sent her a summary of a recent writing of John's on salvation, from which she judged that he had veered from the faith. As they now talked, though, it turned out that the original writing was one Susanna had already read for herself and heartily approved of, somewhat distorted in the retelling, so she again gave him her blessing. Two months later, she herself, while taking Communion, found assurance of God's forgiveness for the first time.

Wesley also saw Whitefield in London, who was preparing to return to Georgia with money he had raised for an orphanage. They went to Whitefield's regular preaching ground at Blackheath, where Whitefield humbly insisted that Wesley preach instead of him. As in Bath, many well-heeled locals turned out and he took the opportunity to address them particularly, driving some but not all of them away with his uncouth bluntness.

Back in Bristol, Wesley was, following a familiar pattern, horrified by how his followers had fared without him: after a week's absence, the groups were in bitter dispute about the 'French Prophets', a group of charismatic Huguenots who spoke in tongues, saw visions and healed. Wesley considered their teachings unbiblical, but rather than immediately joining the dispute he led them in an evening of prayer – his favourite approach to reconciliation – and this succeeded in reuniting the conflicting parties, allowing Wesley to go on and set the matter straight from the pulpit.

Having spent so long defending charismatic activity to his critics as a possible manifestation of the Holy Spirit, he now had to warn his followers that it meant nothing in itself and was only from God if it was accompanied by true biblical teaching. Ironically, his exhortations were punctuated by eight of his listeners collapsing, either shuddering in pain or out cold. Again his follow-up suggested that some had found salvation, while others had just been shown the depths of their sin.

One of the aforementioned critics was Whitefield, who suggested Wesley was giving too much encouragement to this kind of behaviour. Undoubtedly some of it was from God, he conceded, but the Devil was in it somewhere too. Wesley risked making people look more to these signs than to the promises of the Bible. In a revealing question, Whitefield asked 'If I was to do [the same], how many would cry out every night?'

Delayed in sailing to Georgia because of the Spanish war, Whitefield visited Wesley in Bristol in July and they preached around the region together. They discussed these bizarre visitations and it seems that Whitefield's disapproval was somewhat mellowed by Wesley's insistence that he did nothing to encourage them. In an unexpected turn of events, Whitefield himself was preaching the following day – Wesley, significantly perhaps, by his side – when four listeners, one after another, fell down in various states of disturbance. Naturally, Wesley saw the moral of the story: 'From this time, I trust, we shall all suffer God to carry on His own work in the way that pleaseth Him.'

Public antipathy towards the Methodists as a whole was growing.

Newgate Prison closed its doors to them. When Wesley visited Bradford-on-Avon, where he expected to be given somewhere to preach by a gentleman well-wisher whom he had met in Bath, he found that the man had changed his mind after hearing from a mutual associate from Lincoln College that they had always taken Wesley 'to be a little crack-brained at Oxford'. The same day, in Bath, Richard Merchant told him he could no longer let him preach from his grounds because his trees were being vandalized and his things stolen. Wesley had been repeatedly urged by a fan from Wells to come there and use his house. He went in August, sending a message ahead as he went, but before he arrived received a reply: 'Turn back, I beg you, or we shall lose all our trade.' He found someone else to lodge with instead.

In June 1739, something happened that seems inevitable in retrospect, but could only deepen the offence of Methodism and further undermine Wesley's claims to be a model Anglican: a lay society member started preaching. John Cennick had been converted independently and sought out the Methodists in Oxford in late 1738, following Wesley to Bristol, where he became a prominent member and a teacher in the school. Now, while both the Wesleys were away, there was an acute preaching shortage and Cennick – a successful evangelist in private – was persuaded to step in.

When John returned the following week, he faced a dilemma. The Church did not permit lay preaching and it smacked of Dissent and the Puritan revolution, so to authorize it would seriously compromise his defence of Methodism as perfectly within the letter of Church doctrine and law. On the other hand, Cennick had undoubted gifts and Methodism was bound to bring them out – encouraging all disciples to give testimony in meetings, spread the gospel among their acquaintances and maybe take on leadership of their band, was a charismatic process that would sooner or later raise such gifted amateurs. In fact, the Methodist movement as a whole had already embraced them. For example, the Welsh leader Howel Harris himself was – despite repeated applications – never ordained and Wesley had been working with Joseph Humphreys, a Dissenting lay preacher, who in August organized a society of Whitefield's converts in Deptford.

Another consideration is underlined by the fact that Wesley returned to find the society in bitter squabbles after only being away for a week. There was no way he and his brother could be sole leaders and preachers for their growing following and few of their colleagues in the clergy showed any interest in helping. So Wesley gave his permission. In cases of necessity, when no ordained person was available, lay Methodists could preach. Cennick became a 'lay assistant'.

Wesley's attitude to the established Church was clearly being drawn in different directions. He repeatedly met with such undesirables as Quakers and Baptists who, he had to admit, knew the love of God in their hearts. One of the former had belonged to the Church of England until he was troubled by a sense of sin and, asking various ministers for advice, had been told to see a doctor. It was only the Quakers who had helped him turn to the Lord – a story that Wesley retold to shame his Church. However, at the same time, he was exasperated by those among both his opponents and his followers who considered him more or less to have quit the Church himself. Many milder antagonists, such as his brother Samuel, in John's words, conceded that 'I taught no other doctrines than those of the Church; but could not forgive my teaching them out of the church walls'. At the other extreme, many, especially in the less theologically sophisticated levels of society, perceiving him as a disturber of traditional English religion, assumed he was a Roman Catholic. Rumour confidently asserted that he was a Jesuit agent, born and bred in Rome. Wesley insisted that he taught merely the beliefs enshrined in the liturgy and articles of the Church and it was his recalcitrant colleagues who had turned from them. However, traditionalists saw in him a man preaching, outside the Church, doctrines that they had never heard inside it, while his followers looked at the Church and often saw a godless people led by unregenerate priests, united in ritual but not in the Spirit. In fact, some Methodists, including one minister, quit the Church and Wesley was at pains to convince the rest of them that it was necessary for them to stay.

Wesley had been preaching in the fields and streets for six months, gaining some notoriety and hostility for his controversial message and the scandalous phenomena surrounding it. He preached maybe 400 sermons in that time. Charles's preaching was almost as popular as John's and they divided the oversight of London and Bristol between them, ferrying back and forth to cover each other. Extraordinary numbers had heard and extraordinary numbers responded. Most impressive was the tangible transformation that had come over Kingswood in the time that the Methodists had been there. Wesley wrote in his *Journal*:

> The scene is already changed. Kingswood does not now, as a year ago, resound with cursing and blasphemy. It is no more filled with drunkenness and uncleanness and the idle diversions that naturally lead thereto. It is no longer full of wars and fightings, of clamour and bitterness, of wrath and envyings... Hardly is their 'voice heard in the streets'; or, indeed, in their own wood; unless when they are at their usual evening diversion – singing praise unto God their Saviour.

Unfortunately, Wesley was already having some difficulty holding together the divergent tendencies of the new movement, while not being guiltless of divisiveness himself. However, both the hostility from without and the conflict within were pale shadows of what was coming.

CHAPTER 11

STILLNESS AND SCHISM
(1739–41)

'Stand then against your Foes'

From 'Soldiers of Christ, arise'

Why had the Methodists been so astonishingly successful? One thing to remember is the Christian world view of ordinary English people in Wesley's time. The vast majority of them were as confident and unquestioning of the invisible reality of God, sin, judgment and the world to come as their descendants today are of the invisible reality of, for example, human rights. Even the Kingswood populace 'so ignorant of the things of God that they could only be compared to the beasts of the field' probably had a stronger sense of sin than many 21st-century Christians. The fact that they did not live lives in keeping with their beliefs no more undermined them than the same thing undermines today's belief in human rights. Rather, it created a people who knew that they were sinners facing God's judgment, ready to respond greedily to the offer of salvation. The Methodists' emphasis on justification by faith opened a door to heaven for those who despaired of meriting God's favour.

Questions of life after death were sharpened by the reality of the latter. Average life expectancy throughout the 18th century was about 35 years, and many of the stories of Methodist conversions pivot on serious illnesses or bereavements. Over the next few decades, war and the threat of invasion would keep up this impetus.

Then there were the particulars of Wesley's audience. The lives of

Kingswood mining folk were unimaginably miserable – shaped by poverty, squalor, epidemic and endemic disease, industrial illnesses and injuries, violence, alcohol abuse, hunger and cold. Methodism not only promised them that the last would be first, but acted out this message, where the established Church had failed, by treating them as a worthy audience. For those who were abandoned and despised by the world, the message of their value in the eyes of God must have been an uplifting one. Whereas respectable church-goers were frequently offended by Methodists' insistence that they needed new birth before they were acceptable to God, these mining people, untouched by religion, had very little problem with the idea that they were sinners who needed to be saved. The greatest success of Methodism would always be in industrial areas like this, and much of its audience would come from the lower strata of society. It soon came to offer them material provision and a more prosperous way of life here and now as well, though this is jumping ahead of the time we are focusing on here.

The importance of Methodism's willingness to embrace the miraculous and charismatic has not always been recognized, but it was crucial. It was, though by no means uniformly, a religion of dreams and visions, healings, convulsions, ecstatic worship, exorcisms and messages and guidance from God. Such phenomena were exciting for participants and drew many spectators. They were also often decisive in Methodist conversions and played an ongoing part in their spiritual lives.

Obviously the skill of the individual preachers was an essential element too. Benjamin Franklin, who was to be a frequent listener to Whitefield, commented that:

> … every accent, every emphasis, every modulation of voice, was so perfectly tuned… that, without being interested in the subject, one could not help being pleased with the discourse: a pleasure of much the same kind with that received from an excellent piece of music.

Last, but very important, the organization of the societies, especially by Wesley, was essential to the ongoing success of Methodism. They gave converts the support, encouragement and discipline of a religious community, as well as constant evangelical teaching.

The first winter of Wesley's outdoor preaching came, and it was a severe one. The Thames froze solidly enough to hold a fair on its surface. Wesley's ardour was not cooled, though, and the rain did not seem to abate his public's thirst either. From October, he was regularly preaching in the dark, sometimes in sharp frost. In Gloucestershire, he preached for two hours, illuminated only by lightning; in Bradford, he estimated a crowd of 10,000 despite a violent downpour. Materially, though, many of his poorer followers were devastated by the winter as the frost destroyed their livelihood. Some English parishes being adept at evading their duties to the poor, Wesley, as back in the Holy Club days, was moved to start a collection for them. He was able to feed up to 150 a day.

Human hindrances to his mission were as inconsequential as the meteorological ones. His first visit to Wales, at the request of Howel Harris, met with several disturbances, including that of an old man who swore at Wesley throughout his sermon and several times attempted to hurl a stone at him that appears to have been too big for the purpose.

The greatest threat to Methodism at that moment was not its opponents but its adherents: the movement was rocked and torn by an outbreak of 'stillness'. Stillness was a new brand of Moravian teaching introduced to the Fetter Lane Society by the young Alsatian preacher Philipp Molther. He stressed, like others, that we are saved suddenly and completely by God's gift of faith. The difference was that while Böhler had encouraged Wesley to keep preaching even when he knew he had no faith, Molther told people to be still. Until faith comes, in all its instantaneous perfection, they must abandon all the rites of the Church. His thinking was that, as we can ourselves contribute nothing to God's gift of saving faith, then prayer and fasting, Bible-reading, church attendance and Communion, before faith is given, constitute attempts to do God's job for him and save oneself – the infamous salvation by works. According to Wesley (who records the dispute in great detail but also great rancour, so is not at his most reliable), Molther and some of his followers even said that, as nothing pleasing to God can be done by the unregenerate, we should stop trying to do good until we are reliably born again.

Stillness was a bad enough policy, from Wesley's point of view, for those seeking faith, but worse still, many Methodists were joining in who had until now considered themselves believers. Molther visited

Fetter Lane in October 1739 and was first scared and then appalled by their groaning in the Spirit. He told them that they were actually groaning for salvation and had never known true faith. He found them a ready audience and many quit public worship.

Wesley was horrified and insisted that the Methodists continue in active communion with the Church. Less predictably, he turned decisively away from the Moravian understanding of faith that had been so central to his conversion and preaching, to an infinitely more sensible one: faith is not an all-or-nothing windfall, we come to it by degrees. He told the Londoners that they did indeed have faith, however imperfect, if only they knew how to discern it (just as his friends had tried to tell him on his return from Georgia).

Why the change of mind? First, it was not just his own faith that was now in question, but his converts', and questioning this was to question the success of his mission and the validity of his gospel, quite apart from being a pastoral concern. Second, his own experience contradicted Moravian thinking: faith and assurance had come to him not by a sudden infusion, but gradually and imperfectly over a couple of years. Third, what had built up that faith was not Moltheresque quietism, but his relentless missionary activity and the fact that God so obviously blessed it in the form of saving souls. To quote Howel Harris, 'I yet live on distant glimpses, supported by a hidden power to sow the seed.'

Molther was sheep-stealing from the Church of England, robbing Wesley's disciples of their assurance of salvation and pulling away the ladder by which Wesley himself had climbed out of the pit of doubt and anxiety – one that he was still climbing. Molther also embodied those Moravian anti-Anglican prejudices that had so stung Wesley in Marienborn.

In this much, Wesley surely had the best of the argument and the subsequent three centuries of evangelical experience have confirmed his insight that, even for the born again, faith is a journey not an arrival. However, rather than capitalize on this advantage, Wesley squandered it by promoting and inflating his most eccentric doctrine in reply: perfection. His reason for doing so seems to have been that Moravianism left converts with nowhere to go: the 'new man' had been born in them, in all the perfection of Christ, but the 'old man' continued to sin and this is how it would be always until heaven. For Wesley, the struggle to become better than he was, to head towards perfection, was as strong as it ever had been at Oxford and in Georgia (the difference being that now his struggle was carried out against the happy background of assurance of salvation). This drove him, in opposing quietness, to the opposite extreme of insisting that not only progress but perfection was attainable in this life. 'The nature and extent of Christian perfection' became a constant theme of his sermons.

This overreaction doubly aggravated the dispute with the still brethren. It made his basically reasonable position that faith comes by degrees far harder for the dubious to accept and it made him castigate any who denied perfection as antinomians who were happy to accept their sinfulness. This latter point makes Wesley's accounts of Moravian and stillness beliefs frustratingly unreliable.*

Combined with this theological clash was a political one, of course – the struggle for the allegiance of the people and the control of the Fetter Lane Society (and soon many more). If Wesley had been harbouring mixed feelings about the Moravians since his return from Herrnhut, they were now resolving into implacable animosity.

Coming to Fetter Lane again in December, Wesley found the society bitterly divided over the issue, some of them meeting separately with Molther. 'Scarce one in ten retained his first love,' he calculated; 'and most of the rest were in the utmost confusion, biting and devouring one another.' He debated with Molther and preached against stillness, returning to Bristol in January hopeful that he had won them back. He then received a letter from Molther, expressing a prayer that the Lord

---

* After this volume of the *Journal* was published in 1746, a letter was circulated, supposedly from Benjamin Ingham, accusing Wesley of misrepresenting the beliefs of the Moravians and still Methodists and misreporting conversations. Even this letter, however, admits that 'Some of the Fetter Lane Society, when the difference broke out, spoke and acted very imprudently,' though it argues that the Moravians were not to blame. Wesley responded not only by denying the charges, but also with a very direct accusation against Molther. He said that, on 31 December 1739, he told Wesley explicitly that the way to attain faith is not to go to church, take Communion, pray too much, read the Bible or to do good – 'These things I myself heard him speak as I am ready to give upon oath.'

would open up to Wesley the hidden treasure of the gospel. No reply from Wesley survives.

By summer 1740, the Fetter Lane Society was slipping out of Wesley's grip and into Molther's. Visiting in April, Wesley had an acrimonious debate with them. 'Believers', one spokesperson insisted, 'are not subject to ordinances; and unbelievers have nothing to do with them: they ought to be still; or they will be unbelievers all the days of their lives.' He found their meetings dead and the flock filled with 'a harsh, dry, heavy, stupid spirit'. He tried as before to reunite them in prayer, but to no avail. Their 'plague' spread to other religious societies in the London area and to Oxford.

When Molther was taken seriously ill, Wesley declared it the hand of God, but all his impassioned preaching, arguing and imploring failed to capitalize on the intervention. At a meeting at Fetter Lane on 15 July, one member moved that Wesley should no longer be allowed to preach there. A small number objected that his ministry showed the power of God, whereas the Moravians had never converted one soul in England (the Wesleys being two notable exceptions, presumably). The will of the society was clear though. 'We continued in useless debate till about eleven,' says Wesley. 'I then gave them up to God.'

The following Sunday, Wesley came one last time to a Fetter Lane love feast and read a prepared statement. Outlining the stillness teaching to which they had turned, he reminded them how he had called them back from it and shown them how it was contrary to scripture. As they had only grown more convinced in their error, he was giving them up and called all who agreed to leave with him. About 18 came with him there and then and, on the Wednesday, they founded a new society of about 25 men and 48 women. They met in the Foundery in the rundown Upper Moorfields, an old royal factory that had exploded in 1716 and Wesley had bought months ago, converting it into a meeting place in the meantime. Its chapel held 1,500 (the sexes seated separately) and the meeting room 300. The building also contained private accommodation for Wesley.

In all, this was a muddled theological wrangle mixed with power struggle, in which the first casualty was communication and the second was charity.

Among Wesley's faithful flock in Bristol, charismatic behaviour took a new turn in 1740 and, again, it was oddly reminiscent of the modern Toronto Blessing. On various occasions, his followers were taken 'by such a spirit of laughter as they could in no wise resist'. Interestingly, unlike recent exponents, Wesley interpreted the phenomenon as a Satanic attack. Victims were 'buffeted of Satan', 'violently and variously torn of the evil one'. Despite appearances, they suffered terribly but could not resist – unfortunately suggestive of tickling, maybe. Following the usual pattern, Wesley says that those who most emphatically and volubly denied that the laughing was involuntary were taught a hard lesson: they 'were suddenly seized in the same manner as the rest, and laughed whether they would or no, almost without ceasing. Thus they continued for two days.'

Intriguingly, this reminded Wesley of such an attack on himself back in the Holy Club days. As was their wont, he and Charles were taking a Sunday walk in the meadows singing a psalm:

> Just as we were beginning to sing, he burst into a loud laughter.
> I asked him, if he was distracted; and began to be very angry,
> and presently after to laugh as loud as he. Nor could we possibly
> refrain, though we were ready to tear ourselves in pieces, but we
> were forced to go home without singing another line.

What Wesley presents as an isolated incident recalls Richard Morgan's tales of the Oxford Methodists 'laugh[ing] immoderately as if they were mad'. It seems that there was more to this than Wesley was willing to remember.

Wesley's preaching was also increasingly disturbed by opponents. Listeners were assaulted and insulted, but according to Wesley, the thugs were repeatedly won over by the meekness of the Methodists and by power of his words. His first taste of serious mob violence came while he preached in Bristol in April on the plot to kill Paul: 'Not only the court and the alleys, but all the street, upwards and downwards, was filled with people, shouting, cursing and swearing, and ready to swallow the ground with fierceness and rage.' Several attempts by the local authorities to take control failed, until the mayor's officers arrested the ringleaders and dispersed the crowd. (One of the leaders hanged himself a couple of weeks later and another fell painfully ill, which Wesley records in his *Journal*, leaving readers to draw their own conclusions.) Such an outbreak, rather than causing sympathy for the Methodists, only confirmed that their preaching was disruptive and Wesley was immediately banned by the alderman from visiting condemned prisoners at Newgate, even at their own request: 'I cite Alderman Beecher to answer for these souls at the judgment seat of Christ,' pronounced Wesley. Nonetheless, others prisons followed his lead.

In Deptford, a group of prostitutes was procured to disturb the gathering. A rival street preacher in London stole some of Wesley's audience by merely reading a theological text – a hard feat to pull off today. More than once, Wesley came home to find angry crowds lying in wait. He was delighted:

> I rejoiced and blessed God, knowing this was the time I had long been looking for, and immediately spake to those that were next to me of 'righteousness, and judgment to come'. At first not many heard, the noise round about us being exceedingly great. But the silence spread farther and farther till I had a quiet, attentive congregation; and when I left them, they all showed much love and dismissed me with many blessings.

On another such occasion, Wesley ended up leading the crowd in a prayer of repentance.

Wesley seems to have had a quite uncanny ability to disarm (metaphorically) his (often literal) attackers. Over and over, the *Journal* reports that people who came to cause trouble either slunk away sheepishly or stayed to hear what he had to say. Partly, this was the result of his compelling presence. Also, he would immediately address himself to any disturbers, especially to their leaders if they came en masse, and rather than simply berating them, he would preach the love of God to them and pray for them. When he faced really violent crowds, he would try to separate the ringleaders off and subdue them. Often the others would follow their example. His insistence that the Methodists suffer everything without resistance, making no response but to praise God and pray, seems to have frustrated those who came for a fight.

Why were the Methodists facing such ferocity? One reason is the prevalence of mob culture in the 18th century. Ordinary people had no other public voice and little policing, so rioting was their normal (and successful) way of influencing everything from food prices and government policy to the bill of the Drury Lane theatre, and unpopular figures, from lords to pimps and from Scots to homosexuals, were perpetually in danger. In the underclass areas where Methodism thrived, this was especially so. Methodists were seen, not unreasonably, as threatening traditional ways of life: an unknown preacher arrives from nowhere, preaches an unfamiliar message from a makeshift pulpit and persuades converts to attend secret dawn meetings and abandon their 'ungodly' ways of life. Many, from brewers to actors, lost trade because of Methodist conversions and families were split. Catholicism and enthusiasm were feared and hated because of their record in the previous century and Methodism was generally assumed to be one or the other, if not both. There is also considerable evidence that local gentry and clergy organized and paid mobs to disrupt Methodist preaching as they feared both the immediate threat to public order from its large disruptive gatherings and the longer-term threat to the social order posed by letting ordinary people take religion into their own hands.

In the winter of 1740–41, Wesley stepped up the social provision for his followers. He not only distributed clothes among the poor, but also set up a small labour scheme in the Foundery. Thus, 12 of those most in need were taught to spin cotton and provided with spinning wheels. This very much suited Wesley's outlook, because it not only allowed them to be provided for from his meagre funds, but it did so in a way that did not encourage idleness.

Wesley's preaching about perfection was dividing him not only from the Moravians, but also from Whitefield and other predestinarians, confirming for them his wrong-headedness about the doctrines of grace and election. Whitefield wrote to him from Philadelphia in terms of respect, brotherhood and love, but insisted that he was wrong both in his beliefs and the divisive publication of them. 'Why will you dispute?' he cried. 'I am willing to go with you to prison, and to death; but I am not willing to oppose you.'

Others were less reluctant. The person who brought the matter to a crisis was the lay preacher Cennick, who had become close to Whitefield and promoted predestination among the bands at Kingswood. While Wesley was in London in December, Cennick and Charles had a violent falling out over it and preached vehemently against each other. Charles found himself losing the hearts of the flock and offered Cennick a pact of silence, which he refused, so, in a panic, he summoned John.

John talked to the members, trying to heal the 'jealousies and misunderstandings', and preached free will and perfection. However, Cennick preached not only against him but at the same time, leaving John, the mass evangelist, at one point with an audience of fewer than 10. Wesley planned to replace Cennick with the lay preacher Joseph Humphreys, but Humphreys had a mystical experience that turned him into a passionate predestinarian, telling Wesley, 'I now think it my duty no longer to join with you but openly to renounce your peculiar doctrines' (another example of how Wesley's belief about perfection intensified opposition on other issues).

The dispute followed Wesley back to London and, in February, his congregation at the Foundery was leafleted with copies of Whitefield's letter of protest. Taking one to the lectern, Wesley declared, 'I will do just what I believe Mr Whitefield would, were he here himself,' and he tore it to pieces.

Whitefield would have done no such thing. Wesley, to counteract the success of Whitefield's gospel in America, had sent over copies of his published sermon against predestination with an anti-Calvinist hymn by Charles. Whitefield had now read it and was outraged. Writing from his ship en route back to England, he bewailed the Wesleys' decision to start a fight, but insisted he was ready for them. As they were preaching against election, he could no longer preach the gospel without affirming it. He had printed a public reply to Wesley on the subject in which he accused him of pawning his salvation. He also insisted, 'if it occasion strangeness between us, it shall not be my fault'.

Back in London in March 1741, Whitefield pledged to preach election from the rooftops, and was as good as his word. Again, answering Charles's desperate summons, John came and heard his former friend, and talked to him afterwards. John applauded his forthrightness:

He told me that he and I preached two different gospels; and therefore he not only would not join with or give me the right hand of fellowship, but was resolved publicly to preach against me and my brother, wheresoever he preached at all.

This was probably the low point of Wesley's career – his following decimated by losses to stillness on the one side and predestination on the other. It is one thing to face hostile crowds, opposition and physical hardship – Wesley gloried in them all. It is quite another to find yourself at evangelistic war with your closest friends and lose your flock to those you have nurtured yourself. He had to dismiss two of the Bristol school teachers for lack of funds. A natural reaction would have been to regroup, retrench, cut his losses – anything but what Wesley did, which was to start to systematically expel members for unholy living. There can hardly be a better example of his strength of leadership and his sense of divine anointing on it. In the midst of all this turmoil, he made a list of every member in Bristol who had accusations of bad conduct or who simply had no one to vouch for them. He met up with them, along with their accusers where necessary, and if they seemed innocent or repented, he gave them membership cards. Those who failed – 40 of them this first time – were ejected, until they mended. Next time he was in London, he put aside an hour a day for the same kind of discipline and this purging, along with the annual membership cards he now introduced, became a central part of Methodist organization.

He also made the innovation of appointing 12 stewards in charge of social welfare among the London Methodists. It was their job to collect clothes and money (a penny a week per person was suggested) to distribute among those in need, organize knitting work for unemployed women and visit the sick.

CHAPTER 12

OPPOSITION
(1741–42)

'Now it wins its widening Way'
From 'See how great a flame aspires'

As close as they were, there was a great difference in temperament between John and Charles. Charles seems to have inherited their father's passionate volatility, John their mother's sense of reason and order. It tended to be Charles, for example, who was upset by troubles in the societies, and called on John to sort them out. They were both powerful preachers and John conceded that Charles had the stronger turn of phrase – 'all thunder and lightning', as one listener put it – though he himself was better at sustained argument. While they have both been immortalized by their daily writing habits, it is typical of them that John's chosen mode was his methodical, factual *Journal* and Charles chose to write hymns. John also wrote hymns and Charles a journal, but all that survives of Charles's journal is published in two volumes, while John's was published in 24. Equally, John could not compete with Charles's output of hymns, the total of which has been variously estimated at between 4,000 and 10,000.

These hymns were of vital importance to Methodism. They were used to gather crowds for outdoor preaching, they were a popular part of the societies' worship, and they wrote Methodist teaching in the memory of the singers and in their hearts too. They were the most exuberant and emotional hymns that had been written in English, and

John was not above stopping the congregation halfway through to ask them if they really meant what they were singing. They were also weapons in the war over predestination and perfection, and much of Charles's sectarian propaganda survives in hymns sung all over the world today: 'His soul was once an offering made/For every soul of man' is an example of the former from 'O for a thousand tongues', and 'Love divine' is a prayer for perfection.

In 1741, the Wesleys printed *The Morning Hymnbook* for their meetings. As well as Charles's conversion hymns, it included 'O for a thousand tongues', which he had written on the first anniversary of his conversion, 'Jesu, Lover of my soul', 'Christ the Lord is risen today' and 'Hark, how all the welkin rings', of which the first line would later be changed to 'Hark! the herald angels sing'.

Charles, like just about everyone, was more sympathetic to the Moravians than John, and persuaded him to agree to reunion discussions in May 1741 between his Foundery society and Fetter Lane. They prayed together and he was sure that they had heard from God, but the result was not positive: 'It was clear to all, even those who were most desirous of it, that the time was not come.'

There were many other local evangelical missions throughout the country that Wesley remained on good terms with, some led by admirers and converts of Whitefield and Wesley, others that seemed more spontaneous in their origins or predated the evangelical revival. When convenient, Wesley would visit and preach to their societies. Some of the work in the North and the Midlands was sponsored by Methodism's most illustrious adherent, the Countess of Huntingdon, whose servants the Taylor brothers were lay preachers. In June 1741, Wesley went up to Leicestershire to join David Taylor in a preaching tour around the region. We see here the beginnings of Wesley's great 'Connexion' – a national network of Methodist societies united in the Wesleyan gospel – that he would dedicate the rest of his life to building, maintaining and ruling.

On his way north, having often been told by some of his more mystical associates that he should only talk to strangers about God if his 'heart was free to it', he decided to give it a try. The outcome was:

1. That I spoke to no one at all for fourscore miles together…

2. That I had no cross to bear or to take up, and commonly in an hour or two fell fast asleep.

3. That I had much respect shown me wherever I came: every one behaving unto me, as to a civil, good-natured gentleman.

It was certainly a pleasant way to spend the time, but, he decided, hardly one worth making converts to. After two days' journey like this, he returned to his earnest, abrasive self.

In Leicester, he was dismayed to find that Moravian-style Methodism had arrived before him, and preached against it. In Nottingham, he came to address the society and found the meeting room half empty, people chatting instead of praying and, on the lectern, instead of the Wesleys' hymn book and a Bible there were the hymns and sermons of the Moravians. When he opened in prayer, the congregation was taken by surprise and, instead of kneeling, they slouched. The plague had reached there also.

He drew some large crowds, though, and continued to do so when he returned south. In August, he took the funeral of Jane Muncy, one of the most long-standing bandleaders of his London following, outside St Giles, before the greatest multitude he had ever seen.

He continued to suffer isolated attacks from opponents. In Marylebone Fields, amid great disturbance, he was bombarded with stones. They fell to the right and left, but never touched him, so he explained to his visitors that they were servants of a falling evil kingdom, and they swiftly disappeared. He could not always rely on the shield of faith, though, and was once hit on the shoulder by a brick, though he did not note the incident in his *Journal*.

In other parts of Britain, attacks were more serious and Methodism was given its first martyr that year. William Seward was an unusually well-to-do Methodist on the predestinarian side who had donated a lot of the money for building the Bristol meeting house and accompanied Whitefield on his return to America. This time on a Welsh tour with Howel Harris, he was blinded in one attack and killed in a second.

Wesley continued to attack the predestinarians in his own way, but somehow managed to stay friendly with their Welsh counterparts. This was mainly because Harris was devoted to harmony between the two sides – to the extent of letting Wesley think he almost completely agreed with him. When he returned to Wales, he preached alongside Harris and Daniel Rowland, but he found that many unpleasant stories had been told about him that needed to be set right and got into many arguments with those not so committed to peace as Harris.

Wesley covered great distances on his preaching circuit and endured some terrible conditions in the process. He not only preached in rain, hail, sleet, snow and gales, but also travelled on horseback in all weathers. Not surprisingly, he often got lost crossing unfamiliar land in the dark. He had a variety of accidents and frequently suffered various pains and illnesses.

He refused to let these divert him from his mission, though, and repeatedly found that when he forced himself to preach in such circumstances he was not only given strength to keep going but also quite freed from the pain or sickness. Sometimes he specifically prayed for healing so that he could preach and was apparently granted it. On one occasion, his recovery was evidently given as a reward for preaching against the Calvinists. Having spent a day too weak to get out of bed, he dragged himself out to preach:

> Having, not without difficulty, got up the stair, I read those words (though scarce intelligibly, for my voice was almost gone), 'Whom He did foreknow, He also did predestinate.' In a moment both my voice and strength returned: and from that time, for some weeks, I found such bodily strength, as I never had done since my landing in America.

In every circumstance, he saw the hand of God, usually directing the world in Wesley's favour. God sent all rain and sickness and when either cleared up, it was his special blessing. The *Journal* recalls with shame how, lost one night in a downpour, he wished the rain would stop when the true Christian attitude would have been perfect submission to God's will. Once, in October, when his horse fell on him, the locals who helped him turned out to be backsliders whom he was able to recover. 'I adore the wisdom of God,' he reflected.

Over the winter of 1741–42, he was allowed to fall seriously ill.

Repeatedly riding in the Welsh rain and preaching immediately afterwards, he went down with a fever and was bed bound for three weeks. On the worst day of his illness, 'I felt in my body nothing but storm and tempest, hailstones and coals of fire... The fever came rushing in upon me as a lion, ready to break all my bones in pieces.' Even in this, though, there was something to thank God for: 'I do not remember that I felt any fear (such is the mercy of God!), nor murmuring.' Yet he was still upset at how unenthusiastically he welcomed the gift of suffering: 'I found but a dull heavy kind of patience, which I knew was not what it ought to be.'

Deciding, against the doctor's advice, that he was well enough to resume preaching, a week later he was prostrate with fever again. For a couple of months it returned repeatedly, and yet, whenever physically possible, he walked out, frost and rain notwithstanding, preaching and organizing the societies. By the end of January 1742, he had somehow driven himself to recovery.

Strange as it may seem, Wesley was gratified to see violent persecution of the Methodists increasing. A society in Chelsea was attacked through the windows with stones and fire, but Wesley – though ill – was given the strength of voice to rise above the clamour and continued, although no one could see him through the smoke. Such amplified quietism was not enough when the same thing happened in London. The stones and roofing that were coming down made him fear for their lives, so he had a group of burlier Methodists drag the ringleader off to the constable. The troublemakers called on one Richard Smith to take over, but he refused and converted instead.

An outdoor congregation in Pensford, near Bristol, was attacked by a hired gang who tried to drive a bull at them. The bull was an unwilling persecutor and it took an hour to drag him into the crowd. Meanwhile, the Methodists just sang hymns and prayed. Wesley recalls:

When they had forced their way to the little table on which I
stood, they strove several times to throw it down by thrusting the
helpless beast against it, who, of himself, stirred no more than a
log of wood. I once or twice put aside his head with my hand that
the blood might not drop upon my clothes; intending to go on

99

as soon as the hurry should be over. But the table falling down, some of our friends caught me in their arms, and carried me right away on their shoulders; while the rabble wreaked their vengeance on the table, which they tore bit from bit. We went a little way off, where I finished my discourse without any noise or interruption.

Near Whitechapel, his audience was similarly molested with a herd of cows, then stoned. Wesley himself took a stone between the eyes, 'But I felt no pain at all; and, when I had wiped away the blood, went on testifying with a loud voice, that God has given to them that believe "not the spirit of fear, but of power, and love, and of a sound mind".' It was a typically winning display and, from then on, he had the crowd eating out of his hand, so that once again he could thank the Lord for the blessing of suffering for his name's sake.

In February 1742, Wesley stumbled on a new organizational idea that was to prove vital to the long-term success of his movement: classes. The societies were already divided into bands, but these were only for convinced believers, so many society members further back on their spiritual road had no support group. Also, Wesley had no easy way of keeping tabs on them – something he was particularly conscious of now he was regularly trimming numbers. The classes were groups for every member, and their origin was in the debt that Wesley still carried for the building of the New Room. The society there decided that every member should pay a penny a week subscription to build up funds. To organize the collection, they divided into groups of 12, which also enabled better-off members to sponsor others in their group. Wesley immediately found that if he appointed his most reliable people as leaders in each class, he had a system of 'unspeakable usefulness' as the leaders would question, exhort and advise their protégés, and regularly report on them to Wesley.

CHAPTER 13

GOING NORTH
(1742–43)

'Come, O Thou Traveller unknown'
From 'Wrestling Jacob'

Wesley's mission had, until now, been largely confined to the areas around Bristol and London, with occasional forays to other places such as South Wales in support of his allies. However, in 1742, he broke new ground, extending his mission field all the way to Newcastle. It happened almost accidentally. He went to the city for little more than a day, without any apparent plan, but drew such a response that he was soon drawn back.

First, Wesley had business in Leicestershire, going at Lady Huntingdon's request to visit a dying friend. On the way, he started talking to a fellow traveller who was a passionate predestinarian. Wesley tried to avoid an argument but 'he caught me unawares, and dragged me into the dispute before I knew where I was'. A heated debate followed, which culminated in the man accusing him of being one of John Wesley's followers. When he told him that he was in fact Wesley, the man tried to gallop off, but Wesley had the better horse and stuck by his side, explaining the truth of free will all the way to Northampton. Then, after he was finished in Leicestershire, instead of returning to London, he kept going and took a short preaching tour of the North East, accompanied by the lay preacher John Taylor, Huntingdon's servant.

He went first to West Yorkshire. There, his old friend from Oxford and Georgia, Benjamin Ingham, had become another very successful Methodist field preacher, as well as marrying, small world that it is, Huntingdon's sister. However, Ingham was another friend that Wesley had lost in his brawl with the Moravians (in fact, three months from now Ingham was to unite his 40 societies to the Moravian church). Consequently, it was not Ingham that Wesley visited, but John Nelson – a stonemason and self-appointed lay preacher in Birstal who had heard Wesley in London and was expecting his visit having foreseen it in a dream.

Then he went on to Newcastle for a couple of days. Why is not clear, as John had no contacts there, Newcastle being one of the few large centres of population untouched by Methodism. Maybe that in itself was reason enough. Also, the countess had more than once suggested that he should visit the miners of the north. Newcastle was the coal-mining capital of the country (hence the proverbial pointlessness of carrying coals there) and if she thought that Wesley might receive as warm a response from them, as he had from the colliers in the West Country, she was quite right.

Wesley arrived in Newcastle on Friday 28 May 1742 and his first impressions of the city were dire – and therefore most promising. Wherever he went, he saw drunkenness and heard cursing, even from little children. He thought, 'Surely this place is ripe for him who "came not to call the righteous, but sinners to repentance".'

On the Sunday, he walked with Taylor into Sandgate – the most rundown part of Newcastle – and they stood on a street corner and sang a psalm. A crowd soon gathered for this spectacle and Wesley told them about Christ being wounded for their transgressions. By the time he was done, he was surrounded by up to 1,500 people, 'gaping and staring upon me, with the most profound astonishment'.

'If you desire to know who I am,' he said, 'my name is John Wesley. At five this evening, with God's help, I design to preach here again.'

Come five o'clock, the hill was covered with more people than he had ever seen before. He was in good voice, but was convinced that half of them could not have heard him. Nevertheless, he went down well: 'After preaching, the poor people were ready to tread me under foot, out of pure love and kindness. It was some time before I could possibly get out of the press.' He took a different route back to the inn to escape them, but still found some waiting there for him. They begged him to stay a few days, but Wesley had promised he would preach again in Birstal on Tuesday, so he left in the morning. It was a mere taster, but it suited Wesley's palette very nicely.

On the return journey, Wesley visited Epworth for the first time since his father's death. He expected to find all his old acquaintances ashamed of him, but one poor old woman who came to see him in the inn assured him that many in the village had been saved.

His reception at church was more like what he had expected. He told the curate that he was willing to preach or read prayers, but the curate told him that that would not be necessary, and preached himself on the evils of enthusiasm. Afterwards, John Taylor stood in the churchyard as the parishioners were coming out and announced, 'Mr Wesley, not being permitted to preach in the church, designs to preach here at six o'clock.' By six, the largest gathering Epworth had ever seen was waiting for him. Wesley climbed up on to his father's tomb and preached from his favourite text – 'The kingdom of heaven is not meat and drink; but righteousness, and peace, and joy in the Holy Ghost.'

Wesley was persuaded to stay a week, preaching in Epworth and the neighbouring towns and villages. He attracted huge audiences and believed that he was finally reaping the harvest of Samuel's long and faithful but fruitless labours. More than once, he reduced congregations to wailing and convulsions. On his last evening, he had to tear himself away after speaking for three hours. However, the teachings of stillness had taken root there too, and one of the reasons for Wesley staying was to counteract the contagion.

While he was there, locals in a nearby town rounded up a wagonload of Methodists and took them to a justice of the peace. The justice asked what they had done, and according to Wesley's report, the accusers were rather confused by the question:

'Why, they pretend to be better than other people,' one of them answered; 'and besides they pray from morning to night.'
'But have they done nothing else besides?' asked the justice.

'Yes, sir,' said another old man. 'An't please your worship, they have converted my wife. Till she went among them, she had such a tongue! And now she is as quiet as a lamb.'

'Carry them back,' he replied, 'carry them back, and let them convert all the scolds in the town.'

John preached his farewell sermon, once again on his father's grave, and then returned south to resume his rounds.

Later that same month, on 30 July 1742, his mother died at the age of 73. She had been living with Emily in John's apartment in the Foundery and he was there for her last hour. According to his published *Journal*, she was – as he expected any good Christian to be – perfectly calm, and went 'without any struggle, or sigh, or groan', although he had told Charles that she was all the time 'struggling and gasping for life'. While she was either struggling or not struggling, he read a prayer and sang a requiem. He was leaving to get a dish of tea when he was called back just in time to see her open her eyes heavenwards and die. John, with the others gathered there, fulfilled her last request: 'Children, as soon as I am gone, sing a psalm of praise to God.'

Death does not seem to have brought out the best in the Wesleys. The poem Charles wrote for his mother's headstone is an unlovely piece of work. Her entire spiritual life as mother, wife, teacher and disciple, was summed up as 'a long night of griefs and fears,/A legal night of seventy years'. Only three years previously, when she received proper Methodist assurance while taking Communion, was it that 'The Father then reveal'd His Son,/Him in the broken bread made known.'

Similarly, John, writing the day after she died to inform Charles who was not present, had no response more appropriate than self-justification. Having recorded the facts of her going, his only comment is this:

My heart does not, and I am absolutely assured God does not condemn me for any want of duty toward her in any kind; except only that I have not reproved her as fully and plainly as I should have done.

However, he excelled himself writing later that year to his sister Martha Hall, who led a society in Salisbury with her husband Westley, on the occasion of her own bereavement:

> Dear sister
> I believe the death of your children is a great instance of the goodness of God towards you. You have often mentioned to me how much of your time they took up. Now that time is restored to you, and you have nothing to do but serve the Lord without carefulness and without distraction.

On 8 November, John set out for a more substantial visit to Newcastle and stayed until the end of the year. Charles had been there in the meantime, and founded a Methodist society – a 'wild, staring, loving society' as John found it. This was John's first port of call in Newcastle and, throughout his first week, he interviewed each member separately and preached against some of their shortcomings. He found their spiritual progress to follow a curiously different pattern to their southern counterparts: they came on more gradually, without spectacular breakthroughs, and as yet, hardly any were sure of God's forgiveness, but they were also more steady and sure in their progress.

One memorable exception to this rule was John Brown. On 2 December, about half past four in the morning, he was 'raised out of sleep by the voice that raiseth the dead' and filled with love, peace and joy. However, two days later, he 'came riding through the town, hallooing and shouting, and driving all the people before him: telling them, God had told him he should be a king, and should tread all his enemies under his feet'. Wesley sent him back to work and told him to pray for a lowly heart.

There were also occurrences of charismatic wailing and falling down among the Newcastle Methodists. Such things had become a far less common feature in Wesley's *Journal*, though it is debated whether this is because they were not happening or because Wesley felt less comfortable about them. When he does note them, however, he is no more negative than in the earlier days and in later years he reported renewed outbreaks most favourably, so it seems that it was the phenomenon that was waning rather than Wesley's enthusiasm about it. On this occasion he again interviewed those responsible and found that a few had been overwhelmed by their sense of sin, others were merely afraid of the Devil, and many had no clear idea what they were doing. When Charles came the following year, he took firm and successful action to discourage the 'fits'. He suspected their victims of attention seeking, so had them taken outside. Being more class-conscious than his brother, he was pleased to see that this encouraged more of the gentry to come along.

John himself had an experience in Newcastle that he seems to have interpreted as raising the dead or at least the dangerously ill. One Mr Meyrick was given up by the doctor and Wesley arrived to find him cold – to all appearances dead. Along with those in the room, he knelt in tears and cried out to God. Meyrick opened his eyes and called for Wesley, then proceeded to recover from his illness. Wesley makes no explicit claims about this, but adds a characteristic challenge: 'I wait to hear who will either disprove this fact, or philosophically account for it.'

The Newcastle society had grown so quickly that it was already in a position to start building a meeting house. Wesley bought two adjoining plots of land just outside the city walls for a total of £70 and laid the foundation stone. When it was calculated that the building would cost at least £700, many members thought they had bitten off more than they could chew, but he assured them that as they were doing it for God's sake he would provide.

Wesley preached throughout Newcastle for seven weeks, outdoors and in, in frost and rain. He started at five o'clock on his first morning in town – 'a thing never heard of before in these parts', though it was habitual for Wesley. The hospital courtyard proved a favourite place. On the two occasions he visited the village of Horsley, he had to preach outdoors because the room could not hold the crowds. On the second occasion:

> ... the wind drove upon us like a torrent; coming by turns from
> east, west, north and south; the straw and thatch flew around
> our heads; so that one could have imagined it could not be long

before the house must follow; but scarce any one stirred, much less went away, till I dismissed them with the peace of God.

On the way back, he stopped at Epworth once again and preached from Samuel's tomb. This time he was not merely refused permission to preach in church by the curate, but refused Communion. Wesley's response was a classic piece of backhanded vituperation, praising God for this new degree of persecution that could not be more appropriate, coming as it did in his home church and from one who owed everything he had to his father's kindness.

In 1743, his 40th year, Wesley went to Newcastle three times. Throughout the year he extended his weekly preaching circuit to several other mining villages in the area. Chowden was one such, which, for its poverty and irreligion, he called 'the very Kingswood of the north'. He was deeply moved by the sight of filthy, skinny children in rags and blankets: 'They could not properly be said to be clothed or naked,' he said, 'and they looked as if they would have swallowed me up.'

Placey was every bit as bad, its inhabitants 'in the first rank for savage ignorance and wickedness of every kind' and despaired of by everyone. Wesley first went there on Good Friday and, after a 10-mile ride into the north wind and freezing sleet, he could hardly stand. When he had recovered, he preached twice in the town square, in the wind and snow, on Christ wounded for our transgressions.

While there, he was appalled at the way the whole village came together on the Lord's Day 'to dance, fight, curse and swear, and play at chuck, ball, span-farthing, or whatever came next to hand'. Wesley was, in many ways, a harsh saviour. The idea of mining people playing ball on their one day of rest from relentless drudgery and exploitation would seem fair enough to most Christians today. Wesley, however, forbade such recreation to his followers, as he did all secular music and dancing, to the extent that when the miner James Rogers was converted, he immediately smashed up his own fiddle. In Wesley's defence, though, he did not make such rules out of a lofty, cold-hearted disdain for the ways of the lowest classes, but from a powerful sense of compassion for their miserable lifestyles. He saw their problem as a combination of material want, a destructive cycle of drunkenness and violence, and spiritual malaise. Not only was he surely right in this, but he also offered a genuine way out. His societies provided Christian teaching and exhortations from above, but also friendship, encouragement and spiritual check-ups from one's peers. Watchnight services deliberately offered an alternative to worldly celebrations. Equally, Methodist meetings, even if they had little in the way of dancing, were graced with popular hymn-singing.

He went to Sandhill too, because he had seen the poor sauntering about there on the Lord's Day and was moved by the sight. After church, he went up and started singing a psalm. Immediately a crowd of thousands gathered, but simply wouldn't keep quiet enough for him to preach. Even in this, though, Wesley thought the Newcastle ruffians a great improvement on their southern counterparts, as hardly anyone threw anything. However, after an hour's singing and prayer, he gave up and left. He was then banned from Sandhill by the mayor.

In Spen, he found that the way had been prepared by John Brown – the preacher who had claimed to be king. Brown had evidently benefited from Wesley's reproval and his 'rough and strong' sermons had created an open and searching audience. When he returned in November, he found them more moved by his promises than almost any people since his early days in Bristol: 'Men, women, and children wept and groaned, and trembled exceedingly; many could not contain themselves in these bounds, but cried out with a loud and bitter cry.'

Wesley was frequently taken aback by the roughness of Newcastle manners, but he took it all in good part. The idea of their showing approval by slapping him on the back rather startled him at first, though, as did the miner in one of his sermons who, 'not much accustomed to such things', explains Wesley indulgently, began roaring simply for joy at what he heard.

Wesley repeatedly interviewed the Newcastle class leaders to weed out 'unruly walkers' and he expelled 64 members. Almost half the expulsions were for 'lightness and carelessness' and many others for drunkenness. The other faults were railing, quarrelling, swearing, habitual lying, habitual Sabbath-breaking, and selling spirits, with one count of wife-beating and one of laziness. Equally interesting are the reasons given by the 76 members who had left voluntarily in the last 10 weeks. The largest part did so because of the disapproval of their parents, spouses or master or mistress, while many (mainly Dissenters) left because their ministers would refuse them Communion or they were being laughed at. A few were threatened with losing their poor allowance, a few had too little time, two found it too far to come and two did not want to see a particularly annoying member by the name of Thomas Naisbit. One explained that they were frightened of having fits, and another found the people rude; another would not be rebaptized, while another was too loyal to the Church, and yet another felt there 'was time enough to serve God yet'. Such was the growth of the society that even after these losses, they still numbered 800.

Wesley then wrote 'The General Rules of the United Societies' to codify the principles he had been working on. This was an attempt to make sure that he and Charles acted in concert and that the class leaders knew what standards were expected of members. However, he may well have also been thinking in terms of a set of rules by which to unite and integrate the many religious societies run by others throughout the country. That at least was the direction that things were to take from here on. Wesley's takeover had begun.

CHAPTER 14

THE MOB AT WAR
(1743–48)

'Legions of wily Fiends oppose'
From 'Soldiers of Christ arise'

Newcastle, added to his familiar Bristol–London axis, formed the long triangle that was now the basic shape of Wesley's mission. This, in turn, brought other places on the road north into the circuit that he perpetually followed. Epworth became an important centre for him in the East; Wednesbury in Staffordshire was another in the West.

Wesley first visited Wednesbury in January 1743, and his reception augured deceptively well. He preached twice in the town hall to an eager, capacity crowd. He then preached in a large tract of hollow ground outside town that his brother had previously used, first filled with maybe 5,000 people and later the same day with more than it could contain.

On his second visit, though, he had to deal not only with a vitriolic conflict within the society, but with a local clergyman who rode up to their meeting drunk and tried to drive his horse over Wesley's listeners. In June, there were vicious riots against the Methodists and Wesley returned to prosecute the ringleaders. This was a first for him, who had long stuck to the policy of passive endurance as the best example of true Christianity. However, he had a duty to his people as well as his principles and if he feared they were facing a rising tide of violence, his fears were justified.

One evening in October, the Wednesbury mob attacked the house where he was staying, with cries of 'Bring out the minister!' As so often, he somehow managed to disarm them by welcoming in a few ringleaders and quickly placating them. By the time he had addressed the crowd from a chair in the street, many were swearing that they would give their lives for him and only a few hundred were left to drag him off to the justice of the peace. They took him to two justices in nearby towns, both of whom were in bed by this time and refused to see them. They saw one of their sons instead, who asked what their complaint was:

'Why, an't please you,' they answered, 'they sing psalms all day; nay, and make folks rise at five in the morning. And what would your Worship advise us to do?'
'To go home, and be quiet.'

They were doing just this when they in turn were attacked by the Walsal mob, who made off across the town with their hostage. Eventually, Wesley got himself into a doorway and managed to speak to the new crowd for 15 minutes, asking what wrong he had done them, but when he suddenly lost his voice they then dragged him off again.

'Strip him!' suggested some. 'Tear off his clothes!'

'That you need not do,' replied Wesley: 'I will give you my clothes, if you want them.'

Repeatedly throughout the evening, according to Wesley's account, men went to cudgel or otherwise assault him, but inexplicably missed. One came running at him, his arm raised to strike, but at the last moment changed his mind and stroked his head, saying, 'What soft hair he has.' Rioters later told Charles, 'Many blows he escaped through his lowness of stature; and his enemies were struck down by them,' which adds a rather slapstick air to the proceedings. He did take one heavy punch to the chest and another to the mouth that drew blood, but by the power of God, 'I felt no more pain from either of the blows than if they had touched me with a straw.'

They were again hauling him down the street when he found his voice and started calling out in prayer. Suddenly, the leader of the mob turned to him and said, 'Sir, I will spend my life for you; follow me and not one soul shall touch a hair of your head.' Some of his friends followed his lead and they took him back to Wednesbury. The whole ordeal had lasted five hours. When the two justices to whom he had been taken heard about the disturbances, they issued a warrant for Wesley's arrest, but by then he had moved on. The leader of the mob, a man named Munchin, joined Wesley's society: 'He is a man of God,' he said, 'and God was on his side, when so many of us could not kill one man.'

The Wesleys also went to the tin-mining country of Cornwall for the first time in 1743, where the first Methodist society had recently been founded in St Ives by a sea captain. When Charles came in July, he met a mob as violent as those in Staffordshire, who more than once ransacked the meeting house while he was preaching, led by the head officers of the town.

John spent September there. He found that out of a society of 120, 100 had already found peace with God – an unusual blessing that he attributed to their persecution. He received a warm welcome from the tinners, but also his share of violence. When rioters attacked the meeting house, he failed in his attempt to keep the congregation still and so he took the leader up into the pulpit and, after receiving a punch on the cheek, persuaded him to take his accomplices away.

On his last evening in Cornwall, Wesley preached to a crowd of 10,000, and found them so avid, with at least one former attacker in tears, that he could not bring himself to stop until well into the night. Nonetheless, the following morning he was woken at about half past three by a crowd of tinners who would not let him go without a farewell sermon.

By November 1743, Methodism was notorious enough to be satirized on stage. A company at the Moot Hall in Newcastle staged a farce called *Trick Upon Trick; or Methodism Displayed*. One suspects Wesley's account is somewhat overdramatized itself, but apparently, in the first act, the seating on the stage itself collapsed. (In the first half of the century, audiences often sat on the stage, until Garrick's Drury Lane changed the fashion.) In the second act, the shilling seats subsided, while in the third the stage sank and the sixpenny seats fell. Wesley recalls:

Two or three hundred remaining still in the hall, Mr Este (who was to act the Methodist) came upon the stage and told them that for all this he was resolved the farce should be acted. While he was speaking, the stage sank six inches more; at this he ran back in the utmost confusion, and the people as fast as they could out the door, none staying to look behind him.

Which is most surprising – that those players acted this farce the next week – or that some hundreds of people came again to see it?

Britain was at war with France, Prussia and Spain, and there was widespread fear of French invasion, which would doubtless involve the Stuart claimant to the British throne, Bonnie Prince Charlie, the Young Pretender, raising a Scottish army against the English too. As Methodism had always been feared as alien and Catholic, the defensive jingoism of the mid-1740s raised this hatred to a hysterical pitch. In 1744, he was confidently reported to be with the Pretender in France, preparing for invasion, or alternatively in prison as a spy. He was questioned on suspicion of Popery by the justices of Surrey. It was common practice for local authorities in time of war to kill two birds with one stone by rounding up the unemployed and other ne'er-do-wells as military conscripts. This principle was clearly serviceable in the case of Methodists too, and many were seized, including two of Wesley's lay preachers, John Nelson and Thomas Maxfield. Even Wesley himself was taken by an irate gentleman, though he quickly talked his way out of it. On the other hand, Wesley was delighted to correspond with a soldier at Dettingen who was leading a Methodist fellowship in the army.

In Wednesbury, the mob – organized by the gentry and encouraged by the magistrates and clergy – ravaged the house of every Methodist family, taking whatever the rioters could carry and wrecking what they could not. The organizers of the mob offered victims a contract by which they would call off the vandals if they promised to stop bringing Methodist preachers there. 'We have already lost all our goods,' they were told, 'and nothing more can follow but the loss of our lives, which we will lose too rather than wrong our consciences.' To Wesley's outrage, the incident was reported in London newspapers as a Methodist riot.

From St Ives to Newcastle, Methodists were stoned, the women sexually assaulted, their livelihoods destroyed and their houses pulled to the ground. Wesley himself got off pretty lightly thanks to his itinerancy, but he was repeatedly pelted with stones and dirt. His worst moment came in Falmouth, in July 1745, where he went to visit an ill gentlewoman. The house was soon besieged by rioters who forced down the door. The woman made her getaway, leaving Wesley and the servant Kitty with only a wooden partition between them and their unwelcome visitors.

'Oh sir, what must we do?' asked Kitty.

'We must pray,' answered Wesley. Without divine intervention, he did not expect to survive.

'But, sir, is it not better for you to hide in the closet?'

'No,' replied Wesley, who had learnt the importance of the face-off. 'It is best for me to stand where I am.'

A group of pirates took the lead and, playing to type, threw themselves at the door with shouts of 'Avast, lads!' The door fell into the room, and Wesley stepped out into the midst of them.

'Here I am,' he cried. 'Which of you has anything to say to me? To which of you have I done any wrong?' He went up to one after another – 'To you? Or you? Or you?' – until he had worked his way into the street.

'Neighbours, countrymen!' he called. 'Do you desire to hear me speak?'

'Yes,' many insisted. 'No one shall hinder him.'

Those who heard what he had to say were at length won over, but as he had no platform to improve his short stature, they were only a minority. These, however, escorted him down to the sea where he took a boat along the coast. He was not yet safe, though, for his most determined assailants followed him along the shore and were waiting for him when he landed. So, Wesley went up to the first of them, looked him in the face and said simply, 'I wish you good night.' Having pursued him all this way, the man could find no response until Wesley was safely on his horse, when he called after him, 'I wish you was in hell.'

Throughout these troubled times, Wesley kept up with his duties in organizing the societies. He interviewed the members and expelled the unrighteous, reducing the London society first to 2,200 and later 1,900. He made repeated collections of clothes and money for destitute members, who were, of course, increasing in number all the time. His accounts for the winter of 1743–44 show more than 360 Londoners provided for.

In June 1744, he led the first Methodist Conference in the Foundery. In addition to John and Charles, it involved four evangelical ministers (clergymen who agreed with Methodist theology, but less so with their methods) and four lay preachers and they discussed various issues of organization and doctrine, agreeing rules for their societies and the preachers, as well as considering (and rejecting) the possibility of reunion with the Moravians and with Whitefield. They planned to have other such meetings later that year in Newcastle and Bristol, but were not able to meet again until the following August, when there was only one clergyman other than the Wesleys, but six lay preachers. The Conference soon became an annual event for discussing policy and doctrine.

With this small start began a major new development in the history of Methodism. Until now, Wesley had been largely concerned with his own societies in the London, Bristol and Newcastle areas, but recent experience had shown him that other societies across the nation were keen to benefit from his gifts in preaching, organization and discipline. Wesley was delighted to preach the gospel wherever there were ears to hear, but now saw that in return for this he could demand conformity to Wesleyan Methodist rules. The far-flung societies could be integrated into a network, or 'Connexion', and share resources. Wesley could ensure that members and leaders were all doctrinally, morally and organizationally sound.

Wesley had his own personal ills to cope with in these hard times. In 1744, he suffered the greatest pain he had ever felt, which was relieved by preaching. In 1745, he had his worst journey yet, going to Newcastle in 'wind, and hail, and rain, and ice, and snow, and driving sleet, and piercing cold'. 'Oh for ease and a resting place!' he sighed. 'Not yet. But eternity is at hand!' In January 1745, he suffered some kind of nervous crisis. Though he was used to juggling a multitude of troubles, he suddenly felt overwhelmed: 'one, and another, and another, hurrying me continually, it seized upon my spirit more and more, till I found it absolutely necessary to fly for my life'. His idea of a retreat, however, was to go to Bristol, visiting a sick couple on the way, and carrying on his work there.

Those who felt no sympathy with Wesley's religion and the incomparable urgency of saving souls inevitably assumed that he must be in it for the money. A Cornish rector 'calculated' that he made £866,000 a year. Nothing, in fact, could have been further from the truth as, whatever Wesley's faults, greed was never one of them. He despised wealth, dreading its spiritual corrosion, and genuinely preferred giving to spending. He was, indeed, starting to make some money from his writings, but he gave away all that he reasonably could to those in need, leaving for himself merely the wages of an ordinary working man. As his earnings increased, he kept the same amount and just gave more. So, stung by the injustice of rumours that Methodism was his gravy train, he replied to his clerical critics with a splendid, passionate counter-attack:

> For what price will *you* preach (and that with all your might, and not in an easy, indolent, fashionable way) 18 or 19 times every week? And this throughout the year? What shall I give *you* to travel seven or eight hundred miles, in all weathers, every two or three months? For what salary will *you* abstain from all other diversions than the doing good and praising God? I am mistaken if you would not prefer strangling to such a life, even with thousands of gold and silver…
>
> I will now simply tell you my sense of these matters… I have what is needful for life and godliness. And I apprehend this is all that the world can afford… And hear ye this, all you who have discovered the treasures which I am to leave behind me: if I leave behind me 10 pounds (above my debts and the little arrears of my fellowship) you and all mankind bear witness that 'I lived and died a thief and a robber.'

On 25 July 1745, two months after the French victory at Fortenoy, Bonnie Prince Charlie landed in Scotland and started raising an army. Charles Wesley waxed apocalyptic, prophesying 'the Day of Visitation'.

Just as John arrived in Newcastle in September, the news came that the Pretender had taken Edinburgh, and Newcastle was thrown into panic as, with Scotland under the Pretender's control, if he meant to invade England, his next stop would be Newcastle to seize England's coal supply. That night, Wesley preached to a vast crowd on the story of Jonah, where the city of Nineveh was saved from destruction when the people repented of their sin. Then he wrote to the mayor, suggesting that he court divine favour by restraining the ungodliness, drunkenness and profanity of the populace.

The mayor called all householders to arms, set up a guard rota and walled up some of the gates of the city. The Methodists were alarmed that the meeting house where Wesley boarded was outside the city walls, but he assured them that God himself was his wall of fire. He preached long and powerful sermons to responsive crowds in Newcastle and toured the societies in the surrounding countryside.

A spy was captured in the city and was persuaded to divulge the Scots' plan of attack. This allowed the mayor to frustrate it and Newcastle was never besieged. The Scots got as far south as Derby, but were turned back, and in April 1746, were massacred by the British army at Culloden – the last battle still on British soil. With the Jacobite cause finished, and the war overseas drifting into stalemate, the Methodists, although they still had long hard years ahead, had now seen the highwater mark of persecution.

In 1746, Wesley started a fund to give loans to Methodists in need. He lent a maximum of £1 per person, which was to be repaid over three months. In the first year and a half, 255 took advantage of the scheme. He also established at the Foundery the first free dispensary of medicine in London. In its first six months, it gained 300 regular patients, and as many occasional visitors. It lasted for several years, but eventually had to be scrapped because the society could not cope with the ever-growing expense.

Another innovation for the benefit of the poor was that Wesley gave up tea. His talks with class leaders convinced him that poorer members would be much better off not wasting their time, money and health on drinking tea. (On the last point, despite the sanitary benefits of boiling 18th-century water, tea was often blackened with lead.) On going cold turkey, Wesley suffered from a headache and drowsiness for three days, culminating in a bout of amnesia. On the third night, he prayed for deliverance and woke up feeling better.

This sacrifice of Wesley's makes for an interesting point of comparison with the spirituality of his Oxford and Georgia days. Back then, he ardently pursued self-denial merely as a spiritual discipline for its own sake, as if the purpose of creation was to ensnare and be renounced rather than be enjoyed. His life now that he was in his forties was no less arduous, but with the great difference that he had some constructive purpose for his hardships. He lived simply and frugally, travelling on horse and foot in absolutely all weathers. He had no home apart from his rooms at the Methodist meeting houses and the variable lodgings he was given on his travels by members. Neither his dress nor his food was rich. He abhorred idleness as much as ever, filling all his time with preaching, pastoring, prayer and society business – even on horseback he always wrote and read. 'Oh who should drag me into a great city, if I did not know there is another world!' he would cry. 'How gladly would I spend the remainder of a busy life in solitude and retirement!'

In all this, though, he was driving and depriving himself, not as an end in itself, but for the spiritual and practical good of others. 'I love a commodious room, a soft cushion, a handsome pulpit. But where is my zeal if I do not trample all these underfoot, in order to save one more soul?'

In 1746, the Methodist societies of Wesley's Connexion were united into regional preaching circuits. There were seven circuits at first: London, Bristol, Cornwall, Evesham, York, Newcastle and Wales. Wesley divided his preachers into twos and threes and assigned them to circuits for a month at a time. The following year, their annual conference agreed to his rules for preaching:

> Be sure to begin and end precisely at the time appointed.
> Sing no hymn of your own composing.
> Endeavour to be serious, weighty, and solemn in your whole deportment before the congregation.
> Choose the plainest texts you can.
> Take care not to ramble from your text, but to keep close to it, and make out what you undertake.
> Always suit your subject to your audience.
> Beware of allegorizing or spiritualizing too much.
> Take care of anything awkward or affected, either in your gesture or pronunciation.
> Tell each other if you observe anything of this kind.

It is a thoroughly Wesleyan piece of rule-making, dictated by common sense and the needs of ordinary listeners, aiming to keep his largely uneducated lay preachers down to earth and mutually accountable. One assumes that the Wesleys themselves did not consider themselves bound by the second rule.

Wesley extended his preaching to Manchester, Durham and Dublin in 1747, and he drew large, peaceful crowds in each city. His only complaint in Ireland was that those he talked to were almost all Anglo-Irish. Methodism had failed so far to attract native Catholics – hardly surprising considering their treatment by the Church of England. On the other hand, the Dublin society already had 280 members, and they were very teachable – a most important virtue in Wesley's book.

Malicious disturbances continued to attend him in many other places, though. In Shepton Mallet, the curate hired a crowd to interrupt the meeting with a mock psalm and sermon, as well as the more customary stones and dirt. In Leominster, Wesley had to shout over the noise of the church bells and organ. In January 1747, in Devizes, the curate widely advertised a pantomime at the time and place Wesley was due to preach, which backfired rather, giving him a large and eventually attentive audience. The curate learned from his mistake and, the following month, Charles narrowly escaped with his life. In Osmotherly, Wesley met the lay preacher John Nelson, who, the previous day, Easter Sunday, had been seriously injured by a brick to the head, beaten up and left for dead. In Plymouth, Wesley's preaching was disrupted by a mob led by a lieutenant and his drumming soldiers. After 15 minutes of this, Wesley went among the troublemakers, shook one of its leaders by the hand and persuaded him to escort him home.

Returning to Shepton Mallet in February 1748, he was told that a mob had been hired for the occasion, but he preached without disturbance, because it had gone to the wrong address. The rioters found Wesley as he came afterwards to one of the Methodists' houses. A ringleader pushed in and followed him upstairs while the rest outside smashed windows and tiles and tried to break down the door. The leader realized he had made a mistake when an incoming stone gave him a bloody gash on the face.

'O sir,' he panicked, 'are we to die tonight? What must I do? What must I do?'

'Pray to God,' advised Wesley. Wesley, his host and the lone rioter knelt in prayer.

Then, on reflection, Wesley repented having gone upstairs to hide. 'We must not stay here,' he insisted; 'we must go down immediately.'

'Sir, we cannot stir,' replied his host, 'you see how the stones fly about.'

But Wesley was already leaving the room. The other two followed him downstairs, and they were crossing the ground floor when the front door gave way. Wesley records:

Exactly while they burst in at one door, we walked out at the other. Nor did one man take any notice of us, though we were within five yards of each other.

They filled the house at once and proposed setting it on fire. But one of them, happening to remember that his own house was next [door], with much ado persuaded them not to do it. Hearing one of them cry out, 'They are gone over the grounds,' I thought the advice was good; so we went over the grounds to the farther end of the town where Abraham Jenkins waited and undertook to guide us to Oakhill.

Throughout all these reports in Wesley's *Journal*, however, there are growing numbers of occasions where he specifically notes the lack of disturbances, aware that the times seemed to be changing. Even in St Ives, 'we walked to church without so much as one huzza. How strangely has one year changed the scene in Cornwall!... What have we done that the world should be so civil to us?'

CHAPTER 15

LOVE
(1748–49)

'Let us all Thy Grace receive'
From 'Love divine, all loves excelling'

In 1748, Wesley's evangelical faith was 10 years old. It had been broadcast to the nation not only through his sermons but also by a stream of very readable pamphlets. The Connexion that he had built on it now incorporated 80 societies, spreading from Bristol and London down to Cornwall, up through the Midlands to Newcastle and to Ireland, with 21 preachers covering nine local preaching circuits. In the words of Horace Walpole, 'This sect increases as fast as almost ever any religious nonsense did.' Wesley's personal faith was strong – justified, bolstered and saved from introversion by the success of Methodism.

The disastrous romantic entanglement that apparently helped to propel Wesley into his conversion was thus far behind him and there had been no love interest in the story since then. His mission seems to have driven and consumed him enough to guard against any such distractions, in just the way that the Georgia mission had failed to. Yet this work had, at the same time, put him in close contact with hundreds of ardent, devout and admiring women, in increasing numbers, whose company he thoroughly enjoyed. As early as March 1740, a friend had noted, 'John Wesley and Charles are dangerous snares to many young women. Several are in love with them.' These 10 years had not changed Wesley's belief in celibacy. He had recently, for example, published a pamphlet recommending its virtues entitled *Thoughts on Marriage*, which now went to a third edition.* In this respect, a certain Methodist widow would achieve what evangelicalism had not – drawing him into an engagement every bit as messy and unfortunate as the one with Sophy Hopkey had been.

Before that, however, came Wesley's second visit to Ireland. He had heard great things about the growth of the Dublin society since his first visit, which turned out to be wildly exaggerated. According to his reckoning, he had left them with 394 members and found them now with 395. ('Let this be a warning to us all how we give in to that hateful custom of painting things beyond the life,' Wesley reflected.) Altogether, he found that the Spirit flowed in Dublin more broadly and more shallowly than anywhere else. Progress was slow and it was only now that he brought the first society members to the joy of salvation, but almost the whole of Dublin seemed so moved as to desire it. He drew large crowds, including even Catholics now, although on Easter Sunday, the priest came and chased them away.

Wesley was unimpressed to find that preaching did not start until 6 a.m. to encourage more people to come – 'giving place to the Devil', he called it. He preached as ever at five and claimed that it only increased the numbers. As for public mockery of Methodism, he encountered hardly any: 'That is not the custom here... They do not understand the making sport with sacred things; so that, whether they approve or no, they behave with seriousness.' Consequently, he was highly amused to report to Charles how irate the members were 'at a man's throwing a cabbage stalk over a house, which fell at some distance from me. Let them keep their courage till they see such a sight as that at Walsall or Shepton Mallet.' He left Ireland in May, confident that all the work of God yet seen there was 'nothing yet but drops before a shower'.

---

* In 1746, Wesley had admitted to doubts about celibacy being better than marriage, 'which I have not yet leisure to weigh thoroughly', but they were not strong enough to make him revise the pamphlet. The subject was debated at the 1748 Methodist Conference, and his published opinions were criticized. Wesley later maintained that this is when he was finally convinced that there was nothing wrong with marriage. If so, he kept his volte-face well concealed from other conferees, who remembered him being quite intransigent.

He toured England throughout the summer of 1748, with optimistic reflections on the state of play. St Bartholomew's in London and Epworth were both changed places, not least in the case of the latter because the curate had been struck almost dumb. Even in Wednesbury, the crowd behaved impeccably.

In Kingswood, he opened another school – not for charity this time, but to train preachers and give a Christian education to their children. He made the most stringent requirements regarding discipline, timetable and syllabus and over the years would be constantly disappointed on all three counts. The school day was from 4 a.m. to 8 p.m. with plenty of time for religious and physical exercises, including fasting, but no play: 'He that plays when he is a child', Wesley explained, 'shall play when he is a man.'

On 1 August 1748, Wesley was in Newcastle when he was taken ill. He suffered one of his debilitating headaches that lasted almost a week and was nursed by the housekeeper, Grace Murray. She was an attractive widow of 32 and one of the most senior female Methodists. She had been converted in 1739, much to her husband's chagrin, but after he was drowned at sea in 1742 (in fulfilment of a dream she had had), she had become a bandleader at the Foundery. Now back in her native Newcastle, she not only kept house but also taught and examined the female classes and bands and visited the sick and backsliders. She was well-liked, committed and a successful evangelist.

Wesley fell in love with her, but unfortunately seems to have learned little from his faint-hearted dealings with Sophy Hopkey. 'If ever I marry,' he allegedly told her, 'I think you will be the person,' though even this non-proposal comes from his own later impassioned self-defence and the likelihood is that he was even less forthright than this. He claims then to have explained to her that he could not proceed any further without consulting his brother, as he and Charles had promised each other years before that neither would marry without consulting the other.

'It is so great a blessing that I know not how to believe it,' Grace is supposed to have replied. 'It seems all as a dream.'

Wesley recovered from his illness and took a preaching tour of the North West, bringing her at her entreaty as one of the party. She proved 'unspeakably useful'. He was able to observe Grace under fire when they were all assaulted by a mob at the appropriately named Roughlee in Lancashire. At some point he claims to have reprised his overtures to her. 'I am convinced it is not the will of God that you should be shut up in a corner,' he declared. 'I am convinced you ought to labour with me in the gospel. I therefore design to take you to Ireland in the spring. Now we must separate for a season; but if we meet again I trust we shall part no more.' 'I understood him not,' said Grace.

She allegedly promised to marry him and he left her at Chinley in Derbyshire at the house of John Bennet, one of his most valued and successful lay preachers, then headed south.

The reason for scepticism about Wesley's account is that Grace later insisted that she had not the faintest inkling of his feelings for her. It is impossible to say exactly where between the two accounts the truth lies. Wesley, for all his obsession with plain speaking, did anything but when it came to romance. It is entirely possible that he made his feelings less obvious than he thought and later exaggerated how explicit he had been. On the other hand, what follows suggests that Grace may have had her own reasons to be more obtuse or forgetful about Wesley's advances than strictly necessary.

The fact is that she had another suitor – John Bennet, at whose house Wesley had left her. Bennet had also been nursed back to health by her in Newcastle in 1746. Again, what passed between them is hard to ascertain. Bennet later claimed, rather unreasonably, to have taken his recovery as a sign from God that they were to marry. They had certainly exchanged letters and Bennet had apparently talked about marriage, though Grace later claimed, 'I never gave any answer concerning love affairs.'

Now, though, Bennet pressed his suit. More alert to his rival's feelings for Grace than she was herself, the night that Wesley left, Bennet had a vision of Wesley tenderly approaching the tearful woman with the words, 'I love thee as well as I did on the day I took thee first.' Whatever this was supposed to mean, in the dream Grace pushed her dream lover away. In the morning, Bennet told her of his vision.

'Is there not a contract between you and Mr Wesley?' he asked.

'There is not,' she assured him.

Would she marry John Bennet then? She said she would and so, as required by Methodist rules, they each wrote to Wesley for his consent. He did not withhold it, but wrote repeatedly to Bennet trying to dissuade him from the marriage. Bennet assured Wesley he would not marry before they had all three met in person, but insisted that God seemed to him to approve the match.

'I assure you I do not want a woman,' Bennet protested with a gallantry to rival Wesley's own. He thought it right to marry, though, for the greater glory of God and to protect Grace from passions that would be her downfall were they not harnessed by a godly husband (passions she had conscientiously confessed to Wesley too).

Wesley's response was to take Grace to Ireland, a familiarity unusual in the 18th century with a woman of good repute. He had a three-month visit scheduled from April to July 1749 and she came along with a lay preacher to interview and organize the female society members and to help with pastoral visiting.

On the way to Ireland, Wesley took a detour to Garth in Wales to marry his brother. Charles had met Sally Gwynne while he was preaching there in August 1747, when she was 21 and he 40, and he immediately warmed to her. Her father was the justice of the peace, a convert of Howel Harris, and there was some opposition in the family to the marriage because of Charles's erratic income, until John settled £100 a year on him from their combined book sales. Satisfied that the marriage was God's will, Charles entered it wholeheartedly and joyfully, without any of the confusion that disturbed his brother's love life.

The wedding was on 8 April 1749. The sum total of John's comments in the *Journal* are, 'I married my brother and Sally Gwynne. It was a solemn day, such as becomes the dignity of a Christian marriage.' He did provide a rather good hymn for it, though. Charles was a little more forthcoming, writing:

'Sweet day! so cool, so calm, so bright,
The bridal of the earth and sky.'

Not a cloud was to be seen from morning till night. I rose at four; spent three hours and an half in prayer, or singing, with my brother, with Sally, with Beck. And led MY SALLY to church... It

125

was a most solemn season of love! Never had I more of the divine presence at the sacrament...

Prayer and thanksgiving was our whole employment. We were cheerful without mirth, serious without sadness. A stranger, that intermeddleth not with our joy, said, 'It looked more like a funeral than a wedding.' My brother seemed the happiest person among us.

It was to be a happy, successful marriage, however mirthless.

Wesley's third trip to Ireland was an encouraging one, involving extensive touring. At Whitsun, he preached in Limerick Cathedral to a genteel congregation who behaved far better than he had been led to expect and twice in another church, which was packed to overflowing, where he got carried away and kept going for two hours.

Preaching in Athlone, he called on his hearers to give themselves to God and several, including the rector's wife, cried out their assent. Even after he drew the service to a belated close, the congregation would not leave and his attempt to do so himself was foiled by another woman collapsing in anguish and needing prayer. He saw enough responses to the gospel to rebuke himself for taking them for granted:

A few years ago, if we heard of one notorious sinner truly converted to God, it was matter of solemn joy to all that loved or feared him: and now, that multitudes of every kind and degree are daily turned from the power of darkness to God, we pass it over as a common thing! O God, give us thankful hearts.

However justified the rebuke, it clearly illustrates how successful his mission had become. At the same time, he was amazed at how few Methodists here could give an articulate statement of the most basic Christian doctrines. The lesson from this was that God begins his work in the heart and the brain follows later.

Wesley stayed for a week in the vicinity of Portarlington, Queen's County, a town dominated by Huguenot refugees, in which time he found the whole place transformed, immoral behaviour gone and everyone wanting to find salvation. However, experience had taught Wesley that, in most cases, the change would not last. As for anti-

Methodist disturbances, 'What a nation is this!' he exclaimed. 'Every man, woman and child (except a few of the great vulgar) not only patiently, but gladly, "suffer the word of exhortation".' Two days later, he had the opportunity to rethink this opinion when he went through the city of Cork, finding the only way to avoid a riot was simply to keep riding and get out of the town before the mob had time to get itself together. In fact, the city was awash with anti-Methodist violence for many weeks before and after, Methodists being stoned and stabbed, their shops and houses wrecked and burned, though apparently none apart from an unborn baby was killed. The whole county was inhospitable to Methodism, and to the Church of England in general, yet in Bandon (a Protestant town) Wesley preached to the largest audiences he had yet seen in Ireland. He had various rumours and misinformation about the Methodists to correct in these parts, the most extravagant being that 'they placed all religion in wearing long whiskers'.

He went very hoarse in Bandon – 'I could not speak without much difficulty. However, I made shift to preach at nine, at two and at five' – but found that this was when the people most powerfully heard the call of God. He also suffered a cold and facial swelling, which he successfully treated with nettles and warm treacle.

Throughout his three months in Ireland, neither his published *Journal* nor his journal letters to Charles give the slightest hint that Grace was there – though this was quite often the way with his travelling companions. Wesley had the chance to view her spiritual qualities and missionary activities at close quarters and was more impressed than ever. In Dublin, in July, they apparently talked of marriage again and it seems that Wesley convinced Grace that his claims as a suitor had priority over Bennet's, who, he suggested, had probably cooled in his ardour anyway. Apparently, Wesley asked her to marry him and not only did she consent, but they exchanged vows. In common law, this was a binding ceremony.

All seemed settled, but back in Bristol, Wesley, unable to rein in his taste for female conversation, upset Grace with his intimacy with one Molly Francis. Stung with jealousy (according to Wesley), she wrote a love letter to Bennet, promising to marry him. 'Of this she told me the next day in great agony of mind. But it was too late. His passion revived.'

While at Bristol, John and Charles had a meeting with Whitefield and Howel Harris to discuss the possibility of reuniting. This was largely the work of Lady Huntingdon, who, though she was a Calvinist herself and closer to Whitefield, remained on good terms with both sides and repeatedly encouraged efforts towards greater unity. Nothing solid came from the talks, but they seem to have created more friendly feeling between them.

The fundamental difference between Wesley and Whitefield was not the theological one that so exercised them both and sadly caused conflict in proportion to its inscrutability rather than its significance. They were both saving souls and whether that meant harvesting the elect or convincing the free made no difference to how or why they did it. The great difference in reality was one of job description: Wesley was a preacher, pastor, leader, administrator and an architect of religious organization; Whitefield was a preacher. Although he founded some successful 'tabernacles', he had very little interest in organizing converts and left this mostly to others. At the very beginning, this was Wesley, then Cennick and later Howel Harris. Consequently, while there were now over 400 predestinarian Methodist societies in Wales, there were only about 30 in England.

Whitefield had mixed motives for his differing approach: 'Let the name of Whitefield die, so that the cause of Jesus Christ may live,' he said, 'I have had enough of popularity to be sick of it.' He did not want to found a Whitefieldite sect and would rather the movement die of natural causes than be ossified as a monument to him. On the other hand, it seems fair to say that the vast work of nurturing and organizing lacked the glamour of saving souls. He told Wesley, 'I should but weave a Penelope's web if I formed societies... I intend therefore to go about preaching the gospel to every creature.' The result was that, for all his thousands of converts, Calvinistic Methodism did not survive as a significant force in England (unlike in Wales) into the next century. As Whitefield lamented in a moment of self-doubt, 'My brother Wesley acted wisely. The souls that were awakened under his ministry he joined in class and thus preserved the fruits of his labours. This I neglected, and my people are a rope of sand.'

Wesley took Grace on a preaching tour of the Midlands, then they finally met with Bennet in Epworth on 1 September 1749. Wesley laid his cards on the table and, incredibly, this, in Grace's version, was the first moment that she realized Wesley's feelings for her: 'Mr Wesley declared his passion for me which he had conquered too long... I was as much surprised as if the moon had dropped out of her orbit, for I never thought he would marry.' This is such an astonishing statement by someone who, according to Wesley, had gone through a private marriage ceremony with him, that miscommunication is no longer a plausible explanation – one of them had to be simply lying. Long, fiery and tearful arguments ensued over several days, full of pleadings and promises. Grace was torn between two loves, apparently renewing her promises to both separately, and when Wesley left for Newcastle nothing was finally resolved, whatever he might have believed.

Once in Newcastle, Wesley wrote a passionate, vitriolic letter to Bennet:

> You, whom I trusted in all things, thus betrayed your trust, and moved her to do so too... You endeavoured, at a time when I expected nothing less, to rob me of a most faithful and most useful servant...
>
> O that you would take Scripture and reason for your rule instead of blind and impetuous passion!

The letter never reached Bennet, but Wesley did send a copy to Charles at Bristol. This was the first indication he had ever given Charles of his feelings. Finally, he had reached the point of decision – which he never had with Sophy Hopkey – and was now resolute enough to notify his brother of his intentions to marry. It was fatal.

CHAPTER 16

BROTHERS AT WAR
(1749)

'See how great a Flame aspires
Kindled by a Spark of Grace!'
From 'See how great a flame aspires'

Charles, who had so recently entered into the holy estate of matrimony himself, was beside himself with horror at the prospect of John doing likewise. He objected to Grace Murray's low birth, had some reservations about her character and believed her to be engaged to Bennet, but more important, he had a profound and inexplicable terror at the very thought of his brother marrying. He flew into action and rode straight to Newcastle.

At the same time, Wesley and Grace, with others, were leaving Newcastle and travelling west to visit the society of Christopher Hopper in Hindley Hill. They stayed overnight after a highly emotional worship service on 20 September and, in the morning, Wesley received a letter from Whitehaven on the Cumberland Coast with news that revival had washed over the whole town. Answering its appeal, he rode off straight away, leaving Grace at Hindley Hill. However, before he went, at her request, they repeated their vows – this time with Hopper as a witness, to ensure there could be no going back.

Charles, meanwhile, arrived in Newcastle to find John gone. He stayed long enough to hear some very bad reports about Grace from the Newcastle women, and to tell them that his brother was using his 'whole art and authority to seduce another man's wife'. The preachers declared that they would no longer work with him. 'John Wesley is a child of the Devil,' exclaimed one. Another cried, 'If John Wesley be not damned, then there is no God.' One had a dream of him in hellfire. Charles then rode off in John's tracks.

Meanwhile, John was having a wonderful time in Whitehaven. He saw:

… such a work as we have not seen before in England for several years. And it increases daily. Open wickedness is not seen, nor have I heard one oath since I came to Whitehaven. I preach in the marketplace morning and evening. Most of the grown persons in the town attend. And none makes any noise, none laughs or behaves indecently.

He had been there three days when, on 25 September, Charles finally caught up with him. John was quite unprepared for his brother's violent and wild condemnation, not only of John's plans, but also of John himself. John mildly and reasonably explained his position as he saw it, but Charles either would not understand or would not believe him. However, he apparently agreed to let the evangelical minister Vincent Perronet arbitrate.

That night, Wesley sat and, quill in hand, worked systematically through the objections to the marriage felt by himself and others. These would be notes for Charles and their meeting with Perronet. One cannot but raise an eyebrow at the first objection he listed, that he had often said he would not marry 'because I should never find such a woman as my father had'. The suggestion here of Susanna's formidable shadow falling across all of Wesley's relationships with women, undermining them with the impression of her matchless piety and unmeetable demands, is irresistible. His answer to the objection was that he had, in fact, found a few who alone were her equals, Grace being one.

He then considered his earlier belief that celibacy was required by Paul and the early Church, which he now discounted. A more serious problem was that supporting a wife would cost money that he had hitherto given to the poor. His answer was, first, that he already paid for Grace's upkeep and that she would require no more expense as a wife than as a worker and, second, that 'our children (if any) should be wholly brought up at Kingswood' – that is, at the school. The lack of sentiment in Wesley's personal writings is often remarkable, but the coldness with which he embarked on family life is – to modern ears at least – quite chilling.

His greatest concern was that marriage might hinder his preaching. However, Grace was his ideal helper: her housekeeping freed him from menial concerns; she was a tender nurse, 'which my poor, shattered, enfeebled carcass now frequently stands in need of'; and 'as a friend she has been long tried and found faithful' (!). On her gifts as a fellow worker, Wesley waxed ludicrous: she was more used by God than any woman 'in all the history of the Church, from the death of our Lord to this day. This is no hyperbole, but plain demonstrable fact.' She would stoke Wesley's spiritual fire and cool his hasty judgments. Marriage to her would deliver him from 'unholy desires and inordinate affections – which I never did entirely conquer for six months together before my intercourse with her'. Similarly, it would deliver many Methodist women from inordinate affection for him.

Thus, Wesley dealt with all the questions in his own mind about marrying and he then briefly considered the objections of other Methodists too, as he understood them. First, that Grace was low-born: 'This weighs nothing with me, as it does not prevent her grace or gifts.' Whatever respect Wesley had ever had for social class had been eroded by 10 years of field preaching and, unlike his brother or Whitefield, he was only really at home with the lower orders. Second, she had been his servant: 'I like her the better. By that means I know her inside out.' Third, she had travelled with him for six months: 'I should never marry a woman till I had proof that she could and would travel with me.' Finally, he came to the crux of the matter, that she was engaged to Bennet. He insisted, however, that before she promised herself to Bennet in Epworth she had exchanged vows with Wesley in Dublin; and before she had accepted Bennet in Chinley, she had accepted Wesley in Newcastle. Not only was his claim prior, but stronger too: 'At Epworth she only said, "I *will* take you"'; at Dublin she had said, 'I do.'

This is a perfect example of Wesley's tendency to assume that if only he could make a logical case for his position to his own satisfaction, then all would be well. Sadly, however clear he was in his own mind that he was right to marry, the arguments were to no avail. They would have done little to reconcile his disillusioned followers anyway and Charles showed no interest in them. The two of them quarrelled again in the morning, then John went to preach in Keswick. When he came back, Charles had gone.

Charles headed to Hindley Hill, hoping to persuade Grace to come to Newcastle and marry Bennet. John raced through the night, through mist and bog, to Hindley Hill, where he was due to preach anyway. When he arrived, however, he was told, 'Mr Charles left us two hours since, and carried Sister Murray behind him.'

Wesley decided the chase was over. To ride after them, would mean breaking preaching engagements. A friend went instead and Wesley returned to Whitehaven.

He suffered a terrible few days, only feeling at peace when he preached. He resumed his ascetic diet. On 1 October 1749, he asked God to speak to him in a dream. That night, he saw Grace being hanged. She showed no reluctance or resistance and he was equally passive:

> I looked at her, till I saw her face turn black. Then, I could not bear it, but went away. But I returned quickly, and desired she might be cut down. She was then laid upon a bed. I sat by mourning over her. She came to herself and began to speak, and I awaked.

Whatever a modern-day dream analyst might make of this, Wesley interpreted it as a word from the Lord that the affair was finished and he was to put to death all hope. He spent the following day in prayer and fasting, remarking, 'We had free Access to the Throne of Grace, & I found my Will more resigned.'

The next day, called by Whitefield, he went to meet Charles in Leeds, only to find the latter refusing to see him until Grace and Bennet were married. John was distraught and Whitefield prayed over him with tears and tried to comfort him without success. Wesley considered his suffering to be God's punishment for his divided loyalties and supposed slackness in preaching.

On Thursday, a messenger from Newcastle arrived saying that Grace and Bennet had been married on Tuesday. According to his own account, Wesley accepted the news quietly for all his inner grief, but Bennet said, 'he was so enraged as if he had been mad'.

Charles arrived, calmer now, but still bitter: 'I renounce all intercourse with you,' he told John, 'but what I would have with a heathen man, or a publican.' Whitefield, again in tears, saw Wesley's Connexion being destroyed and implored Charles to reconsider, but John accepted the estrangement. 'It was only adding a drop of water to a drowning man.'

Then Bennet arrived on the scene. Wesley burst into tears and they kissed. This display of fraternal solidarity achieved what nothing else had, finally persuading Charles to listen to his brother's defence. John once again explained his side of the story, they agreed that the whole thing must have been the woman's fault and on that basis were reconciled – although in truth their relationship never wholly recovered.

So the sorry affair drew to a close, although bitter exchanges continued between Wesley and Bennet. What are we to make of it all? The one thing we can say with confidence is that we cannot know what passed between Wesley, Bennet and Grace, and latterly Charles, let alone what their motives were. The information we have is partial, in both senses, and where we have two people's accounts of the same events the conflict between them is repeatedly so great as to cast grave doubt over the uncorroborated accounts too. This misrepresentation, obfuscation and dishonesty make an unedifying episode all the more discreditable. Biographers and editors have tended on the whole to follow Wesley's version, which is especially tempting because it is fuller and more complete than the others, but Wesley was a partisan witness at the best of times and in his own personal maelstrom of passion and betrayal, where his whole credibility among Methodists and that of Methodism before the world were at stake, it is naive to assume that his recollections were reliable – they were not even entirely consistent. He felt passionately for Grace and considered himself betrayed by her and Bennet, and that is about as much as we can know for certain.

CHAPTER 17

MARRIAGE
(1750–51)

'Let me to thy Bosom fly'
From 'Jesu, lover of my soul'

The end of Wesley's first notable romance with Sally Kirkham immediately preceded the great burst of religious fervour in 1725 that some have called Wesley's real Christian conversion. Later, when the affair with Sophy Hopkey ended, he was thrown into the spiritual turmoil that culminated in his evangelical conversion. One cannot help wondering if there was more to this than coincidence, if romantic frustration and sexual disappointment fuelled his spiritual crises. With Grace Murray, however, there was no religious upheaval on the rebound from romantic passion. Instead, he rebounded into another romantic misadventure. It was as unlucky as the others, not because it failed but because it succeeded. Less than 18 months after Grace and Bennet were married, so was Wesley. If the match was made in heaven, it was arranged to some other end than Wesley's domestic happiness.

During those 18 months, Wesley continued his preaching, pastoral duties and oversight of the Connexion, as he had almost without pause throughout the crisis with Grace. Lady Huntingdon made another attempt to bring the Wesleys and the predestinarians together and this time it seemed to work well. Whitefield and Harris visited Wesley's London chapels several times in January 1750 and joined with Wesley in preaching and leading prayers.

'How wise is God in giving different talents to different preachers!' was Wesley's somewhat barbed, though genuine compliment to Whitefield on one of these occasions. 'Even the little improprieties both of his language and manner were a means of profiting many who would not have been touched by a more correct discourse, or a more calm and regular manner of speaking.'

He paid a fourth visit to Ireland from April to June. Again, his presence in Cork provoked riots and he was burned in effigy. He preached at a great Methodist funeral, which proved to be quite an education:

> I was exceedingly shocked at (what I had only heard of before) the Irish howl which followed. It was not a song, as I supposed, but a dismal, inarticulate yell, set up at the grave by four shrill-voiced women who (we understood) were hired for that purpose. But I saw not one that shed a tear; for that, it seems, was not in their bargain.

Due to the difficulty of finding lodgings, Wesley once ended up riding 90 miles in a day – a record even for him.

On his return, after preaching to huge congregations in Cornwall, Wesley spent much of the winter editing and rewriting books for the Kingswood school – from Latin grammars to *Foxe's Book of Martyrs*, in the latter case reckoning to rescue some venerable records from a vast heap of trash.

As Wesley tells it, he had been discussing with the minister Vincent Perronet whether or not it would be a good thing for him to marry and, on 2 February 1751, finally decided to do so. The Lord had allowed him to stay single until now and he had believed himself to be more useful to him this way, but now Wesley thought he would do better with the support of a wife. They also decided who the woman should be – the 41-year-old widow Molly Vazeille.

Molly Vazeille was of Huguenot descent, had four children and had been left rather well off by her husband, a London merchant, who had died four years previously. Charles's first impression of her when they had met in 1749 was of 'a woman of sorrowful spirit'. At today's distance she seems a strangely faceless person – only three letters of hers survived the Methodist shredders.

Charles's reaction to the news of his brother's intentions was what can only be described as a sulk. He was again horrified by the idea, even before he heard who the bride was to be. 'Groaned all the day and several following ones,' he wrote in his *Journal*. He refused food, refused to go to meetings with John and, when he celebrated the Eucharist, refused to sing or lead in prayer. He shut himself up 'to mourn with my faithful Sally', presumably oblivious to the hypocritical irony.

The reason for Charles's implacable, desperate opposition to John's marrying anyone can only be guessed at. Perhaps he felt some kind of dependence on John that would be hurt by marriage. Certainly his own rationalization – that he feared for the flock who would be left without a shepherd – is insufficient. However, the contrast could hardly be greater between his passive misery in this case and his whirlwind offensive against the match with Grace. One would like to think that, after that disaster, he was ashamed to interfere again, although there must have been a limit to the number of times one can marry off someone's fiancées anyway, and John was clearly not going to give him the chance to do so this time.

Wesley followed up his engagement, in his inimitable fashion, with an address to the unmarried men of the Foundery, urging on them the value of celibacy, though also explaining that 'a particular case might be an exception to the rule'. He was then due to ride north, but he slipped on the ice on London Bridge and sprained his ankle. A surgeon bound up his leg and he walked to the West End and preached. Not surprisingly, even after he was taken back to the Foundery in a sedan chair, the pain was so great that he could not preach.

So, he spent the week at Molly's house, reading, writing and once again testing the nursing abilities of his intended. Then, forced to abandon his plans for the next preaching trip, he married her. Precisely when we do not know, as one newspaper announced it as Monday 18 February and another as the Tuesday. As to where we have no idea. All we know is that Charles was not invited, only hearing about it several days later, and that presumably John was not able to stand up as, on the Sunday, Tuesday and Wednesday he preached in the Foundery kneeling.

One of his fears in marrying Molly was that he would be suspected of doing it for her money. Avarice was the last accusation that could be justly made against Wesley but, to protect his name from slander, he legally settled her income on herself and her children.

He left them in March to visit Bristol for the eighth Methodist Conference. Although Charles was feeling too petulant to attend, he thawed enough to visit Molly and, when John returned, they were more or less reconciled. John's earliest surviving letter to his wife from Bristol is full of affection, but the greater part is given over to preaching. The opening words reproach her for not writing, he declares his growing love for her ('God grant it may never go beyond his will'), then:

> Do you neglect none of your temporal business? Have you wrote to Spain? Have you sold your jewels?... Do you not forget the poor? Have you visited the prison?... I want you to crowd all your life with the work of faith and the labour of love. How can we ever do enough for him that has done and suffered so much for us?

John stayed for a week and then rode off for a two-month trip north, preaching and examining the preachers of his Connexion. 'I cannot understand how a Methodist preacher can answer it to God to preach one sermon or travel one day less in a married than in a single state,' he insisted. 'In this respect surely, "it remaineth, that they who have wives be as though they had none".' Such a comment, one month into his marriage, shows how unfounded Charles's fears were that a wife would divert John from his calling, but it hardly augured well for the success of the union.

Preaching throughout the Midlands, Wesley was delighted by the large numbers who came to hear, their warm response and the lack of disturbance in places such as Wednesbury and Birmingham, which had been so perilous for Methodists before. In Dudley, they were at first greeted by the 'dismal screaming' of their opponents, but nothing more violent than that.

More upsetting news was that the region had been on the receiving end of a campaign by Wesley's predestinarian rivals. Venturing into the Midlands for the first time, they had drawn away many of Wesley's members – the Wednesbury group was reduced to a quarter of its earlier size. Not only had there been furious disputes between the rivals, but many had left the Church of England for the Baptists, broken out into 'the wildest enthusiasm' or had been guilty of backsliding altogether – for all of which Wesley blamed the predestinarians. The sight of those who, in Charles's words, had 'borne the burden and heat of the day, and stood like a rock in all the storms of persecution, [now] removed from their steadfastness, and fallen back into the world, through vain janglings' was heartbreaking.

Wesley was refreshed by a visit to the 'loving, simple and zealous' people of Newcastle, then he went on to take his first trip to Scotland. He went diffidently, not expecting to preach, and only for a couple of days, believing his suspicions of the Scots to be more than reciprocated. However, he found prejudices on both sides were easily overcome and was equally easily persuaded to preach. His only criticism was that Edinburgh was one of the dirtiest cities he had ever seen. An elder of the kirk and a magistrate implored him to stay, but he was expected elsewhere and could only promise to send one of his preachers. On his way back to London, he stopped at Epworth and found it just as badly hit by predestination as the Wednesbury area, and riven by dissent against the rules of his societies.

Wesley spent most of the rest of the year with his wife, taking her, after six weeks at Bristol, on a typically demanding tour of Cornwall. Even while they were still in Bristol, Charles found her in tears and had to listen to her complaints about John. He tried his hand at marriage guidance and left the pair of them, he believed, in 'perfect peace'.

A problem that weighed more heavily on the Wesleys was the scandalous behaviour of one of their lay preachers, James Wheatley. Wheatley was a phenomenally successful evangelist in the West Country, but in June, Charles heard reports that he had been committing some kind of sexual improprieties with a string of female Methodists in the area of Bradford-on-Avon. He got the whole story from the women concerned, then he and John, along with two of the women, confronted Wheatley. Wheatley confessed, but insisted that they were only 'little imprudences', of which many other Methodist preachers were equally guilty, threatening to expose them all.

They suspended him 'from preaching and from practising physic' until the next Methodist Conference as a token of repentance, but he refused to stop. He preached against the Wesleys and those preachers he accused of misconduct. The Bristol society was divided by the scandal, but when John and Charles brought him face to face with those he accused, it seemed he had no accusation to make and so he was generally dismissed as a liar and went off to Norwich.

However, while Wheatley's sins seem blatant from the Wesleys' accounts, once again the truth is veiled by mixed reports. Many, not least Whitefield, defended Wheatley as the honourable victim of salacious gossip: 'Sinners [have been] convicted,' said Whitefield, 'saints edified, and my own soul sweetly refreshed.' Wheatley had a devoted, though violently victimized, following throughout his life.

John's response to the affair was to embark with Charles on a tour of inspection to examine the life and teaching of every preacher in their Connexion, and a major purge followed. Again, Charles rather fell out with his brother over this. He wanted to get rid of a number of preachers who simply were not terribly good, but John insisted that they needed 40 preachers to maintain the Connexion and that grace was more important than gifts.

Charles, like several of their preachers, was getting annoyed by John's autocratic rule, so he went ahead and, without John's consent, dismissed one preacher John had appointed. 'A friend of ours', he said (about his brother) to John Bennet, who shared his resentment, '(without God's counsel) made a preacher of a tailor; I, with God's help shall make a tailor of him again.' He also spent money setting preachers up in business for the express purpose of making them less dependent on his brother (although he himself was dependent on John's writing for the money with which to do so). As he told Huntingdon, 'it will break his power, their not depending upon him for bread, and reduce his authority within due bounds'. Unfortunately, this letter found its way into John's hands, with predictable results.

As far as John was concerned, submission to his autocracy was the quid pro quo for the benefits of belonging to his Connexion and the only way to keep his colleagues walking in the one true way (he himself being the only reliable cartographer of the one true way). Joining Wesley's Connexion was very much like being bought out by a national corporation. Preachers who had been running local societies and overseeing local revivals then took on the Wesleyan franchise and could avail themselves of the regular preaching visits of Wesley and his men, his expertise and authority in disciplining and administering the society and they benefited from his good name. However, in return, they were expected to surrender all independence, conforming absolutely to rules on doctrine, organization and lifestyle. This McDonaldsization of Methodism was extremely successful, but it was often resented by the preachers and there was a constant falling away. One of the more vociferous dissidents was Bennet, who finally renounced Wesley's Connexion in December 1751. 'After he had said many bitter things of [Wesley] to the congregation at Bolton,' reported one of them, 'he spread out his arms, and cried, "Popery! Popery! Popery!"' The success of Wesley's franchise is demonstrated by the fact that after this schism it was he rather than Bennet who managed to keep charge of most of Bennet's flock.

CHAPTER 18

THE VALLEY OF THE SHADOW
(1752–55)

'Dark and cheerless is the Morn'
From 'Christ, whose glory fills the skies'

Molly found being Mrs Wesley hard to get used to. When John took her on his travels she could not bear the hardships that he hardly noticed; when he did not, she felt neglected. She was repeatedly upset by John's relationships with others, especially women. 'My wife,' as John put it, 'upon a supposition that I did not love her, and that I trusted others more than her, had often fretted herself almost to death.'

After wintering down south with his family, John set off in March 1752 for a four-month tour of the North and the Midlands. Molly and her daughter Jenny came with him and he told a friend, rather optimistically, 'the more she travels the better she bears it'. She stuck it out for six weeks before returning to Bristol where her sons had been taken seriously ill. Before she left him, Molly had her first true taste of anti-Methodist violence when John preached for the first time in Hull. Several thousand came to hear, but many pelted them with stones and clods. They made an unusually grand and undignified exit: a gentlewoman invited them into her coach, but this meant nine passengers, crammed between two seats. They were bombarded through the open windows as they left, 'but', said John, 'a large gentlewoman who sat in my lap screened me, so that nothing came near me'. They were deposited at a friend's house, but there a mob of thousands found them and attacked the house repeatedly throughout the evening.

When Molly returned to Bristol, John wrote to her, condemning himself for wasting the time he had spent with her. 'The thing which I feared has come upon me. I have not conversed with you so seriously as I ought... We should be as guardian angels to each other... And can I laugh or *trifle a moment* when with you? O let *that moment* return no more!'

It is debatable whether or not Wesley had any real sense of humour at all. His writings often display a monstrously grim attitude to laughter. In a letter of rebuke to his brother-in-law Westley Hall in 1747, he lists among his complaints, in between Hall's heresy in denying the afterlife and his marital unfaithfulness, the fact that he 'could break a jest, and laugh at it heartily'. Wesley even complained about Whitefield's conversation 'being often mixed with needless laughter'. Yet the former Methodist John Hampson remembered Wesley's manner thus:

> It was sprightly and pleasant to the last degree and presented
> a beautiful contrast to the austere deportment of many of his
> preachers and people, who seem to have ranked laughter among
> the mortal sins. It was impossible to be long in his company
> without partaking in his hilarity.

Perhaps his doing was more human than his teaching.

In June 1752, John paid his first visit to Chester, preaching to maybe 10,000 in the square, including many of the gentry. He was pleased with the response, despite a few small disturbances. During his first sermon, 'one single man, a poor ale-house keeper, seemed disgusted, spoke a harmless word, and ran away with all speed'. However, a week after he left, the Methodist meeting house was pulled to the ground by rioters.

For three months in the summer, Molly and Jenny accompanied John around Ireland. Apart from the fact that the women were extremely sick on the ship, their visit was pleasantly free from trouble – a fact that John put down to the shock of several anti-Methodist rioters having been recently brought to trial. His greatest concerns were that spiritual discipline, sobriety and doctrinal soundness were in decline. When he chastised his Irish preachers for this, he was less than happy to be met with the defence that his brother let them get away with it. A stinging letter to Charles followed.

In 1753, as Wesley turned 50, he returned to Scotland and went for the first time to the Isle of Wight. A couple of his *Journal* entries for that year show that neither the bizarre religious phenomena of Methodism nor Wesley's interest in them were quite dead. First, there was one of his Connexion who had the gift of preaching in his sleep. He would sing a hymn, recite a text and then preach a six-point sermon, sometimes breaking off to dispute with a clergyman who came to interrupt him.

Then there was a 10-year-old girl of Woodseats near Sheffield who suffered demonic fits for five months. At first the fits were either of violence or laughter, but they grew more outrageous. She tried to throw herself into fires or out of windows. She tore off all her clothes, screaming, 'Save me! Save me! He will tear me to pieces', 'He is tearing off my breasts; he is pouring melted lead down my throat.' She shouted curses and shocking blasphemies and tried to tear up the Bible. She had visions of heaven and hell and Wesley coming to visit the house. However, by the time he came, she had finally recovered.

Also around this time, one of Wesley's lay preachers, Thomas Walsh, had a charismatic experience so far apparently unique among the Methodists – speaking in tongues: 'This morning the Lord gave me a language that I knew not of,' he recorded in his diary, 'raising my soul to him in a wondrous manner.'

In October 1753, Wesley fell seriously ill in London. He suffered from fever, heartache, shivering, cramp and coughing. His remedy was to try and shake it off with a preaching tour of Kent, with unhappy results. In November, he took the advice of a Quaker doctor and rested at Vincent Perronet's in rural Shoreham, riding daily and drinking asses' milk. He soon felt much better, but returning after a week to the Foundery he was immediately as bad as ever. He preached twice on the Sunday, as the services were for charity and had been advertised in the papers, but in the evening, preaching on 'Who shall change this vile body?', he was barely audible. It was obvious to the congregation that he was dying. Nevertheless he went on to a society meeting afterwards.

Again the doctor insisted that he needed rest and country air, so on Monday he took a coach to the wholesome pastures of Lewisham. He stayed with his friend Ebenezer Blackwell, whose country house was a favourite retreat when he needed to escape the stress of city life and concentrate on his writing. That night, he wrote an epitaph for his tombstone:

> Here lieth the body
> of
> John Wesley,
> a brand plucked out of the burning:
> who died of consumption in the fifty-first year of his age,
> not leaving, after his debts are paid,
> ten pounds behind him:
> praying,
> God be merciful to me, an unprofitable servant!

Whitefield had seen the state he was in in London and now wrote a touching farewell letter to him:

> The news and prospect of your approaching dissolution hath weighed me down. I pity myself and the Church, but not you – a radiant throne awaits you, and ere long you will enter into your master's joy. Yonder he stands with a massy crown, ready to put it on your head amidst an admiring throng of saints and angels. But I, poor I, that have been waiting for my dissolution these nineteen years, must be left behind to grovel here below!... If prayers can detain [the chariots], even you, reverend and very dear sir, shall not leave us yet... My heart is too big, tears trickle down too fast, and you I fear, [are] too weak for me to enlarge. Underneath you may there be Christ's everlasting arms.

Methodist leaders had often discussed what would happen to the movement after Wesley's death, without coming up with an answer. Now the question became urgent, but the only apparent successor, Charles, utterly refused to consider it. The fact is that there was simply no one in the movement who combined both Wesley's ability and energy. From this perspective, his autocracy seems more understandable, though his unwillingness to share the reins did itself make it harder to raise up new leaders.

Thankfully, Wesley recovered over the course of the next six months, a blessing he rather churlishly ascribed not to the doctor's orders but to a concoction of sulphur, egg white and brown paper that he was miraculously inspired to try. He did a great deal of writing, drank regularly from the Hot Well in Bristol and, by March 1754, was able to preach again, but it was over a year before he regained his strength. Consequently, for the first time in 12 years he spent the whole year in the South.

The main concern he had to deal with during his convalescence was dissident preachers. The annual Conference expelled William Darney, for example, for persisting in preaching predestination and printing dreadful poetry in the belief that it was inspired by God. Others were lost to the Anglican and Dissenting ministries and still others were 'persuaded' by Wesley to join other Methodist groupings because they would not agree to stop contradicting him from the pulpit. John Edwards was expelled after he refused to give up the Leeds house and chapel. He had been a very successful travelling evangelist, but then wanted to settle in Leeds. Wesley had granted him only a six-month long probation there because of his predestinarian tendencies, but afterwards he refused to move. The house and chapel were successfully repossessed and Edwards, taking a number of the congregation, set up a flourishing independent meeting house.

In July, John and Charles had to go to Norwich where the alleged philandering preacher Wheatley was again kicking up the dust. The abuse suffered by his followers was terrible even by Methodist standards. In addition to the typical riots and the demolition of their meeting house, a woman was gang raped, a pregnant mother kicked to death and another person was whipped through the streets wearing a crown of thorns. Wesley was sympathetic, but put the blame for this persecution on Wheatley's shocking waywardness, much as the public blamed the Methodist sufferings in general on Wesley.

By the time Wesley's marriage was in its fourth year, it was in trouble. April 1755 brought the long travelling season round again and, more or less back to strength, John took Molly on an extensive tour of the Midlands and the North, including his first trip to the rapidly growing port of Liverpool. She complained about the food, the rooms, beds, roads. To John's dismay she was even so unspiritual as to malign God's gift of foul weather. 'I am discontented with nothing,' he told his confidant Blackwell in Lewisham. 'And to have persons at my ear fretting and murmuring at everything is like tearing the flesh off my bones.' Naturally, he bore this trial contentedly too, but 'to hear his government of the world continually found fault with (for in blaming the things which he alone can alter we in effect blame him), yet is such a burden to me as I cannot bear without pain; and I bless God when it is removed'. He was impatient with her and not willing to compromise the work of the Lord for a woman's weakness. Once, when a coach was waiting to take them to a preaching engagement and she was not ready, he waited 10 minutes watch in hand, climbed aboard, and left her behind. She opened his letters, one to a Mrs Lefevre convincing her that they were committing adultery. She and Charles would no longer speak and she accused the brothers of conspiring to keep her out of their way. Though this was not true, when John left her in London in August, going to Cornwall alone, he said, 'I leap as broke from chains.'

CHAPTER 19

DISSENT
(1755–58)

'Indissolubly joined'
From 'Soldiers of Christ, arise'

Methodism having been a nonconformist denomination for over two centuries since Wesley's death, it takes an effort of historical imagination for us to see it as it was in his eyes – a campaign to revive and restore the Church of England. Wesley was, as we have seen, a devoted son of the Church for whom Dissent was an indefensible error. Yet in his later years, Wesley himself led the Methodists to the very exit of the Church.

Nothing could have been further from Wesley's intention, but neither was it merely a historical accident. The great paradox of Methodism is that, while Wesley was a passionate supporter of the established Church and the purpose of the movement was to revive it, the movement was fundamentally at odds with its principles, being a voluntary gathering of a minority of 'true Christians' into congregations for teaching, worship and fellowship, writing off the mass of baptized church-goers as 'almost Christians'.

Wesley did everything he could to ensure that Methodists attended the parish church, especially for the Eucharist, and that they did not think of the society as a church, but the dynamic of the movement was against him: Methodism was, de facto, a church within the Church and, considering the hostility of the Church to it, it was only a matter of time before it became a church outside the Church. Even Wesley's promotion of the Eucharist hastened the division, as we shall see below.

His attitude to the Church had become increasingly complicated. He took every opportunity to protest his loyalty to it and dissociate himself from Dissent, yet he respected Dissenters and their Puritan forebears and no longer believed episcopacy to be the one form of church prescribed by the Bible. He allowed his preachers to visit their pulpits – 'The *place* does not *make the dissenter*' – and though he was not so outspokenly ecumenical as Whitefield, the title of his 1753 book *Hymns and Spiritual Songs Intended for the Use of Real Christians of All Denominations* speaks for itself. Dissenting churches were now warming to Methodism too. Having originally denounced it out of anti-Anglican prejudice and the survival instinct of an already sufficiently persecuted minority, their ranks were now swelling with evangelical converts unwilling to stay in the Church.

His commitment to the Church of England, however strong, had in fact been conditional ever since his conversion. From the start he was clear that if, God forbid, he was forced to choose between submission to the Church authorities and obedience to his divine mission, he must serve God rather than man. This was another point of conflict between John and Charles, because their ultimate priorities were different. For Charles, *reviving* the Church of England was not as important as being *in* the Church of England; for John, the revival was more important than the Church.

There was pressure on Wesley from Methodist ranks, including the preachers, to make the break and become a separate church, and Wesley was coming to have considerable sympathy with them. Their most pressing concern was the Eucharist as few ministers shared Wesley's enthusiasm for it, so many Methodists had to travel long distances to receive it with any kind of frequency and sometimes they were turned away from the Lord's table. The vast majority had to receive it from the hands of non-evangelical priests, men they considered unregenerate and often impious. Many of the clergy attacked Methodism in print and from the pulpit and, indeed, attacked Methodists physically, either in person or with hired mobs. Why, their victims felt in increasing numbers, should they not take Communion from their own preachers? They had their own meetings, their own worship, their own teaching – all greatly preferable to what the parish had to offer – so why not their own church, so that their preachers could be ordained as ministers and administer the sacraments? After 17 years of the Methodist revival, it was becoming clear that the Church was not going to embrace evangelicalism and Methodists increasingly felt that it was thus effectively separating them from itself, whether they wanted this or not. Ironically, they would be better protected under law as Dissenters, being eligible for preaching licences.

In 1755, the issue came to a crisis. The previous autumn, the Methodist lay preacher Charles Perronet (the son of the evangelical clergyman Vincent Perronet) had given Communion to some of the London flock. Charles Wesley was appalled and demanded that John discipline him. According to Charles, John was not greatly troubled and suggested that this was the logical conclusion of appointing lay people to preach: 'We have in effect ordained already.'

John was persuaded by the militants to devote the entire Leeds Methodist Conference of 1755, their largest yet, to a three-day debate over whether or not they should separate. In his keynote speech, he listed the arguments in favour of separation and rebutted each one and eventually persuaded all 62 preachers present to agree to remain within the Church. (To ensure unanimity, Perronet was not invited.) However, this practical restraint was only achieved at the cost of a huge concession of principle: their agreement was that 'whether it was *lawful* or not' to separate, 'it was in no ways *expedient*' to leave now. John was impressed with their peaceable humility, but Charles walked out in disgust, announcing, 'I have done with conferences forever.'

John also established with his preachers an agreement that they would not administer the sacrament. The concession rankled bitterly with Perronet and he quit the Connexion. 'Here is Charles Perronet,' groaned Wesley, 'raving because his friends "have given up *all*", and Charles Wesley because they "have given up *nothing*".' To the latter, John insisted that he would seek no further concessions from his preachers until they came round to the Wesleys' own way of thinking. 'And I am not in haste for that.'

On the other hand, going on to Newcastle, John was dismayed to find that a number of the society had already quit the Church, believing that he had given his consent, and many more were on the point of following. After an uplifting Whitsun celebration in St Andrews ('God has not yet left the Church'), he spent a week interviewing the society one by one and, he hoped, persuading them to stay.

The Church itself did nothing to encourage Wesley's loyalty. In June 1755, the Bishop of London for the first time excommunicated one of his lay preachers for preaching without a Dissenters' licence. 'It is probable the point will now speedily be determined concerning the Church,' John said to Charles. 'For if we must either *dissent* or *be silent*, it is all over. Adieu.'

He wrote for advice on the matter to some evangelical clergymen and, inevitably, they urgently pressed him to stay. They even encouraged him, as did Charles, to appease the Church and woo the public by cutting back field preaching, putting an end to lay preaching and having his preachers ordained. Wesley, however, rejected this concession out of hand. Even assuming his preachers would be accepted into the ministry (a large assumption), they could never reach nearly so many people settled in a parish. There were 34 societies scattered across Cornwall alone – how could they all be served without itinerant preachers? Wesley reckoned that few evangelical clergy had achieved any conversions at all in their parishes. Congregations soon get bored of hearing the same voice. What rights would 'valid' ordination gain his lay preachers anyway? Surely these men, who were evidently called by God, had more right to preach the gospel than any recalcitrant vicar who was merely called by the Church authorities and did not even know what the gospel was: 'Soul-damning clergymen lay me under more difficulties than soul-saving laymen!' Following the evangelical clergy's advice would make Methodism more respectable and less effective – not a trade-off that filled Wesley with enthusiasm.

In fact, their discussions only impressed on Wesley what a strong case for separation his preachers had. Could he, in good conscience, require Methodists to receive the ministry of men who denied that there was any such thing as being called by God, to listen to their false teaching, hear them subvert the gospel and thereby encourage others to give ear to them? His rebel preachers disparaged Church laws – 'the very dregs of popery' – and the requirement on ministers to declare that every word of the prayer book was in harmony with the Bible. Wesley could not disagree with them.

No, there was no question of turning back to conformity; the only question was whether or not he had yet turned far enough from it. However, when it came to the crunch, he could not bring himself to separate from the Church, unless he was thrown out. It could only be right to leave, he told himself, if it was against God's law to stay and that point had not yet come. However, he had to admit that he had not answered his preachers' arguments to his own satisfaction: 'My conclusion, which I cannot yet give up, "that it is lawful to continue in the Church", stands, I know not how, almost without any premises that are able to bear its weight.'

The following year, 1756, while John spent most of the summer in Ireland, Charles toured England preaching Anglicanism to the societies and, in his own words, following the troublesome preachers around 'with buckets of water'. The campaign was a fraught one and proved to be the last of his itinerant ministry. He then settled down in Bristol and gave up travelling.

The arrival on the scene of John Fletcher was good news for everyone involved. A former Swiss mercenary, he was converted to Methodism while he was employed as a tutor in Shropshire in the winter of 1753–54 and took to preaching. With Wesley's encouragement, he was ordained in the Church of England in March 1757 and immediately became Wesley's right-hand man. Gifted, saintly and a priest, Fletcher was exactly the kind of recruit Wesley was looking for and, although they remained very close, it was a grievous disappointment to Wesley that, in 1760, he joined the ranks of evangelical Anglican clergy and settled down in the parish of Madeley in Shropshire.

Another significant placement of 1757 was Sarah Ryan, whom Wesley appointed as the new housekeeper at Kingswood in November. His marriage having been on the rocks for most of its duration, this godly Methodist would soon be the unwitting agent of its shipwreck. Sarah, now 33, had been converted by Whitefield at 17 and, a couple of years later, married a bigamist. She later went on to marry another couple of men concurrently herself. She was reconverted by Wesley in

1754, and it was a mark of his confidence in, and affection for, her that only three years later he was, despite various warnings, taking the risk of putting her in such a responsible and prominent position.

'On what a pinnacle do you stand!' he warned Sarah, in a letter hardly calculated to fill her with confidence. 'You have no experience of these things, no knowledge of the people, no advantages of education, not large natural abilities, and are but a novice, as it were, in the ways of God! It requires all the omnipotent love of God to preserve you in your present station.' This rather makes one wonder why Sarah was appointed. Molly Wesley also found it incomprehensible and put it down to impure motives on John's part. During the 1757 annual conference at Bristol, she burst in as Sarah was serving dinner to the assembly, crying, 'The whore now serving you has three husbands living!' She was bitterly suspicious of John's relationship with her and, in response to her allegations of adultery, she claimed, John barred Molly from Communion for several years.

Wesley exchanged many letters with Sarah over the next couple of months. His were naturally full of preaching, making demands that were sometimes ridiculous in their extremity:

> Do you never find any wandering thoughts in prayer or useless thoughts at other seasons?... Is there no vanity or folly in your dreams? No temptation that almost overcomes you? And are you then as sensible of the presence of God and as full of prayer as when you are waking?

They also contained some fearsome warnings for Sarah: 'I can hardly avoid trembling for you still. Few persons in England can have been in so dangerous a situation as you are now.' However, these were balanced with many protestations of confidence, admiration and affection from Wesley: 'You have refreshed my bowels in the Lord; I feel your words, and praise God on your behalf. I... love your simplicity.' 'Your letter came in a seasonable time, as rain in a time of drought. How fain would we excuse those we love!' 'I know not whether any was so regarded both by my brother and me at the same time. What can I do to help you?' and 'The conversing with you, either by speaking or writing, is an unspeakable blessing to me. I cannot think of you without thinking of God. Others often lead me to him; but it is, as it were, going round about; you bring me straight into his presence.'

The letter containing these last words was seized by Molly before it was sent on 20 January 1758, the day that she announced she was leaving her husband. Oddly enough, and contrary to what is generally supposed, finding the letter does not seem to have provoked her to walk out, but rather had the reverse effect. She announced that she was leaving him because of genuine grievances about her marriage and unfounded suspicions of infidelity. John, of course, then went out to preach as normal and, while he was gone, Molly returned to search his correspondence for evidence of adultery. The letter, for all its intimacy, contained nothing worse and so, filled with contrition, she renounced for the moment her suspicions and leave-taking and stayed.

It was the wrong decision. It would have been better for everyone involved if John and Molly had never seen each other again. After her decision to leave, John had 'almost doubted' if he was right to be so free in his correspondence with Sarah, but now he saw Molly's repentance as God's sign of approval. Her accusations and fault-finding quickly returned, however, and within two weeks he was complaining to Sarah of 'the being continually watched over for evil; the having every word I spoke, every action I did (small and great) watched over with no friendly eye; the hearing a thousand little, tart, unkind reflections in return for the kindest words I could devise'.

Molly broke into John's bureau and took letters and other writings. Although she found nothing genuinely incriminating, there were suggestive passages in his correspondence not only with Sarah Ryan but also with Sarah Crosby – a 29-year-old deserted by her husband who had become a class leader at the Foundery. Molly was enraged and showed them to anyone who would look as evidence of her husband's treachery. John's friends took the middle ground, encouraging him to stop writing such letters to mollify her. 'I certainly will,' protested the furious John:

> ... as long as I can hold a pen, assert my right of conversing with
> whom I please. Reconciliation or none, let her look to that. If the

unbeliever will depart, let her depart. That right will I exert just when I judge proper, giving an account only to God and my own conscience.

All the same, he made a free and independent decision to suspend communication with Sarah Ryan and Sarah Crosby. This cheered Molly up, but the suspension was short lived and so was the cheer.

Wesley spent the summer of 1758 on a tour of Ireland, where the controversial phenomenon of congregations wailing for salvation became all the more controversial by being led by children. 'I hope I shall see your wicked face no more' were Wesley's parting words, according to Molly – words he violently denied having spoken. He wrote to her several times without reply and found letters forwarded to him from London already opened. Reunited in England, they clashed violently – Wesley refusing to change his writing habits and Molly accusing him of adultery and calling down on him, in her own words, 'all the curses from Genesis to Revelation'.

CHAPTER 20

PERFECTION
(1759–63)

'A Heart from Sin set free'
From 'O for a heart to praise my God'

For almost as long as he had preached faith, Wesley had preached perfection. He passionately believed that the Bible promised the Christian life could be free from sin. He had written and preached on the doctrine and fought for it at length. It was a theoretical point that had proved terribly divisive and caused much ink to be spilt without having had any obvious practical relevance to anybody's life in 20 years – until now. At the end of the 1750s, some Methodists started to claim that this long-contested 'second blessing' had actually happened to them. By 1760, the perfectionist revival was sweeping the societies across the nation.

The first instances seem to have come in 1758, but Wesley was more interested for the moment in a remarkable local revival in Everton. It was led by a couple of Anglican evangelical ministers, John Berridge and William Hicks – the latter only just converted – and it revived the charismatic spectacles of earlier Methodism on a scale not seen since those first few years. When Wesley preached there in 1759, listeners cried aloud and collapsed. At other times they saw visions and received revelations, suffered violent convulsions and contortions, their faces went red or black and they went into trances or passed out altogether, sometimes for hours at a time. Mrs Blackwell told Wesley of a well-dressed visitor opposite her who:

... fell backward to the wall, then forward on his knees, wringing his hands and roaring like a bull. His face at first turned quite red then almost black. He rose and ran against the wall, till Mr Keeling and another held him. He screamed out, 'Oh what shall I do? What shall I do? Oh for one drop of the blood of Christ!'

There were also outbursts of laughter reported, though, unlike in Bristol in 1740, they were welcomed as expressions of the joy of salvation (except when they interrupted a sermon). Another oddity was that a high proportion of those affected were children and teenagers. Wesley investigated and was intrigued and impressed. He read an account of these meetings to the York society and was delighted that it provoked similar reactions.

The perfectionist revival seems to have been triggered by an intensified focus on the subject by some of his preachers. Already in 1758, he was having to counsel (rather irritably) a woman in Bristol who was upset by hearing preachers apparently claim, 'A believer till perfect is under the curse of God and in a state of damnation.' Wesley rejected this teaching, but did not distance himself very far from it. He proclaimed, he told her, the gift of 'perfect love' – that is, 'loving God with all our heart, so as to rejoice evermore, to pray without ceasing, and in everything to give thanks'. Also, though believers without such perfection are in a state of grace, nevertheless 'till you are saved from unholy tempers you are not ripe for glory. There will, therefore, more promises be fulfilled in your soul before God takes you to himself.' The gift of perfection could come gradually or instantaneously. He discussed the doctrine with his preachers at Conference and it was agreed that perfection, paradoxically to say the least, can coexist with 'imperfections'.

By 1760, the Everton extravaganza had tailed off and Wesley started to travel the country investigating the rapidly multiplying claims of perfection. He interviewed two in Wednesbury. This was the testimony of one of them:

About Christmas, 1758, I was deeply convinced there was a greater salvation than I had attained. The more I saw of this, and the more I prayed for it, the happier I was. And my desires and hopes were continually increasing for above a year.

[After being told by a preacher she/he might receive it that night] I felt God was able and willing to give it then, and was unspeakably happy. In the evening as he was preaching, my heart was full, and more and more so, till I could contain no more. I wanted only to be alone, that I might pour my soul out before God; and when I came home I could do nothing but praise and give thanks. From that moment I have felt nothing but love in my heart; no sin of any kind. And I trust I shall never more offend God. I never find any cloud between God and me: I walk in the light continually.

In Leeds, Wesley interviewed many from the surrounding towns who now committed no sin and lived in continual love and communion with God. Was this 'sinless perfection'? 'I do rejoice, and will rejoice, call it what you please.'

Did Wesley himself receive the gift of perfection? He makes no statement in any of his writings, leaving us to weigh up the probabilities. On the one hand, could he have preached and promised perfection so fervently if he had never known it himself? The answer to this is, knowing Wesley, very possibly, just as he preached faith in 1738 'until he had faith'. If he had received it, on the other hand, would he not have broadcast the fact? This is not so sure. Wesley was not in the habit of illustrating his written sermons with examples from his personal life and on this subject more than any other it would have made him a hostage to fortune. However, when one considers how unreserved the *Journal* is about his evangelical conversion and the wonderful changes that made in his life, it does seem strange that he should make no mention at all of attaining a 'greater salvation'. In 1767, he did say on the letters page of *Lloyd's Evening Post*, 'I have told all the world I am not perfect.' That, however, was many years later and was not necessarily intended to disclaim ever having known 'perfect love'. On balance, however, the likelihood is that he had not received it.

Wesley's private life was far from perfect at this time. He saw little of his wife and received no letters from her. He gave her the benefit of his plain speaking, writing to her with a list of the faults he wanted her to mend and wishing her 'the blessing which you now want above any other — namely, unfeigned and deep repentance'. He had a bureau built with secret compartments to hide sensitive papers from her. A short reconciliation was demolished in March 1760 with a row over whether or not she should put a dismantled bed in his study. He exploded:

> Alas, that to this hour you should neither know your duty nor
> be willing to learn it! Indeed if you was a wise, whether a good
> woman or not, you would long since have given me a carte
> blanche: you would have said, 'Tell me what to do, and I will do
> it; tell me what to avoid, and I will avoid it... Bid me do *anything,*
> *everything.*'

Almost the sole surviving record of this marriage from Molly's side dates from December 1560, when she said Wesley left a meeting early with one Betty Disine and was seen still with her the following morning. She told him 'in a loving manner to desist from running after strange women for your character is at stake'.

His relationship with his brother was as bad as it had ever been. In February 1760, three Methodist preachers in Norwich started to give the Eucharist to their members and others had applied for Dissenters' preaching licences in an attempt to avoid persecution. John could not be bothered with this old chestnut and refused to deal with it until the August Conference. Charles threatened to renounce Methodism if this Dissenting behaviour continued and rounded up a like-minded party. The crisis blew over simply enough when, at the Conference, John gently persuaded the Norwich preachers that they were breaking the rules of the Connexion and to give it up.

Immediately afterwards, however, Methodism took another step away from Anglican orthodoxy with the advent of women's preaching. Wesley had from the start given women more responsibility and authority than they had ever had in the Church of England, appointing them as leaders of bands and classes and he encouraged them as much as men to spread the gospel among their personal acquaintances. In

1761, Sarah Crosby, the London class leader whose letters Molly Wesley had commandeered, went a step further when she was sent to Derby to oversee the female classes there. When 200 members turned up she could not interview each separately, so, reluctantly, she addressed them from the front, telling her own story and urging them to flee from sin.

She continued the practice and wrote to Wesley asking if it was wrong. Wesley felt some scruples about biblical and ecclesiastical standards of propriety, but his deepest instinct was that if it was useful for the spiritual lives of his people, God could not object. Sarah cannot have gone too far, he decided, as she could not in conscience have done any less. He suggested:

> When you meet again, tell them simply, 'You lay me under a great difficulty. The Methodists do not allow of women preachers; neither do I take upon me any such character. But I will just nakedly tell you what is on my heart.'... I do not see that you have broken any law. Go on calmly and steadily.

The same year, he encouraged one Grace Walton to give her women 'a short exhortation' when necessary and offered her some exegetical guidance in getting round Paul's apparent prohibition of female teaching.

This is typical of the way in which Wesley dealt with such issues. Whether he admitted it or not, he was a pragmatist and questions about lay sacraments, separation from the Church and women preachers were ultimately decided by what worked best for the Methodist revival. 'Necessity has no law,' he said. His concession to propriety was to call what the women did 'exhortation' instead of 'preaching' and to present it as a temporary expedient, a contingency plan, and he always reconciled his practice with the letter of the scriptures (and where possible Church law). However, it was in reality neither propriety nor the Bible that ultimately made his mind up, but the practical needs of the work of the Lord.

By the time Wesley left London in March 1761, he reckoned 15 or 16 had been perfected there. By August, every society in the area had caught the fire. Throughout the year, Wesley travelled round the country preaching perfection and hearing the stories of those who had attained it from Bristol and Canterbury, through the Midlands and across Yorkshire and Northumberland. In Bristol and Wednesbury, perfection blossomed almost daily. Wherever it happened, though, there were knock-on effects, with others being converted for the first time and believers who had fallen away being reclaimed.

Experience increasingly persuaded him that it came as a sudden dramatic transformation, just like saving faith. Also like faith (at least like faith in the early days), it was often accompanied by the same kind of supernatural phenomena. A woman in Whitby, only 18 days after her conversion, 'was convinced, in a dream, of the necessity of a higher salvation' and she received it five days later. A woman in a London meeting, Wesley recalled,

> '... began to tremble exceedingly, and soon after sunk to the floor. After a violent struggle, she burst out into prayer, which was quickly changed into praise. She then declared, 'The Lamb of God has taken away all my sins.' She spoke many strong words to the same effect, rejoicing with joy unspeakable.

The one area that notably failed to receive the blessing was Wesley's beloved Newcastle. He had a ready explanation, which he put in their own mouths:

> 'We see now, we sought it by our works; we thought it was to come gradually; we never expected to receive it in a moment, by faith, as we did justification.' What wonder is it, then, that you have been fighting all these years as one that beateth the air?

By the end of the year he was reflecting:

> It seems God was pleased to pour out his Spirit this year on every part both of England and Ireland, perhaps in a manner we have never seen before, certainly not for twenty years. Oh what a pity that so many, even of the children of God, did not know the day of their visitation.

Naturally, perfectionism faced considerable opposition from within the Methodist movement. Wesley's preaching and arguing won round many doubters; some others he expelled for preaching against it. Predictably enough, passions and denunciations became heated on both sides and the doctrine of perfect love proved to be another source of bitter conflict.

This kind of controversy was only to be expected in championing such an eccentric doctrine, but far worse lay around the corner. What turned the perfectionist revival from a dream come true for Wesley into a nightmare was Thomas Maxfield. Maxfield, whom we have met once being press-ganged in 1744, was one of Wesley's first lay preachers – according to some the very first – but certainly the first regular lay preacher. At any rate, he was a man for whom Wesley had stuck his neck a long way out. They had worked together for 20 years, in which time Wesley had persuaded the Bishop of Dublin to ordain him, introduced him to his wealthy wife-to-be, made him his deputy at the Foundery and helped him out of a number of scrapes. It was while Wesley was praying with him that he had been first saved and Wesley had a deep paternal love for him.

So, it was alarming when Maxfield started to take the doctrine of perfectionism to new extremes that even Wesley could not accept, and a cruel blow when he then started preaching against him. He teamed up, in 1761, with a sanctified former corporal named George Bell, claiming that they were now incapable of wrongdoing or even being tempted, having been restored to a more pristine condition than Adam and Eve. They gathered a following in London, encouraging them to see visions and hear messages from God and abandon prayer as they were now constantly in the divine presence. They believed that they could read the state of people's souls and rarely liked what they saw, condemning as godless virtually everyone other than their own clique. Their meetings were high-powered charismatic affairs, with 'screaming', several people praying at once, leaders whipping the people up to cry out 'I believe!' and claim their perfection and, according to Wesley, 'poor, flat, bald hymns'. Ultra-sanctification also gave them healing powers. Wesley himself believed that Bell had healed a woman of breast cancer, though his attempt at the more readily falsifiable achievement of sight to the blind certainly failed. It was also revealed to Bell that the world would end on 28 February 1763.

The immoderately perfect condemned ordinary Methodists as thoroughly as the Methodists condemned the 'almost Christians' of the Church of England, and complained of persecution from the Methodists as the ordinary Methodists did from the unregenerate Anglicans. Wesley was slow to act against them, both because of his love for Maxfield and also because he reckoned 80 Methodists in London had been genuinely justified by this work. Throughout 1762, Wesley laboured to persuade Maxfield of his error and ingratitude, but Maxfield's answer was that he did not care 'if you call me John or Judas'. It was no easier to convince him of error than it was Wesley.

In February 1763, Maxfield and Bell quit the Foundery and 'Blind John's Connexion', taking with them 100 to 200 members. However, even those who rejected their doctrine were worried about the end of the world they foretold, so, on the day Bell had picked (while Bell himself was locked up in case he took the apocalypse into his own hands), Wesley preached on the text, 'Prepare to meet thy God', explaining that the Day of Judgment could not possibly come that night, though of course one could die at any time:

> But notwithstanding all I could say, many were afraid to go to bed, and some wandered about the fields being persuaded that, if the world did not end at least London would be swallowed up by an earthquake. I went to bed at my usual time and was fast asleep by 10 o'clock.

The saddest result of the Maxfield–Bell affair for Wesley was that it did a great deal to discredit perfectionism among Methodists and the wider world. The perfectionist revival as a whole had passed its height by the time of Maxfield's secession and it would doubtless have tailed off soon enough by itself as such things do. Wesley was never disillusioned by it, though. He continued to preach instant perfection for the rest of his life and recorded many successes throughout 1764. He learnt one lesson, however, as he saw the sanctified return to their previous lives:

Formerly we thought, one saved from sin could not fall; now we know the contrary. We are surrounded with instances of those who lately experienced all that I mean by perfection. They had both the fruit of the Spirit, and the witness; but they have now lost both.

CHAPTER 21

THE HORRIBLE DECREE (1764–71)

'For every Soul of Man.'
From 'O for a thousand tongues to sing'

The remainder of the 1760s were relatively uneventful years for Wesley. Now himself in his sixties, he made not the least concession to age and simply continued business as usual, riding across England, Wales, Scotland and Ireland in all weathers, covering 3,000 miles and preaching 800 sermons every year, outdoors and in. 'It pleases God', he said, 'that I, who am now in my sixty-third year, find no disorder, no weakness, no decay, no difference from what I was at five and twenty, only that I have fewer teeth and more grey hairs.'

The Connexion now had more than 30 preaching circuits, with a few less than 100 itinerant preachers, and the total number of society members increased by the end of the decade to almost 30,000. Nearly a quarter of them were in Yorkshire. The London societies had 2,250 members in 1767, significantly fewer than before the perfectionist revival. Cornwall, Newcastle and Lancashire each had in the vicinity of 2,000, Bristol about half that number. Wales had a few more than 200 Wesleyans, Harris's predestinarian Methodism having triumphed there, Scotland twice that figure, and Ireland nearly 3,000.

Wesley continued constantly to make rules for the Methodists – in particular for his preachers. A major concern these days was how to remain on good terms with the Church, to which end he gave them a nine-point plan: they must go to church and encourage the people to go; they should take the sacrament whenever possible; Methodists must be warned against 'the great and prevailing evil' of being too choosy in hearing parish preachers and taught not to despise parish prayers; they must not be allowed to call the Methodist society 'church', the preachers 'ministers' or the preaching houses 'meeting houses'; and the preaching houses must not be licensed as Dissenting chapels.

He passed rules through Conference concerning every area of preachers' lives and work. They should preach every morning and evening, but 'not too loud or too long' and 'not lolling with your elbows'. No sermon should start after 7 p.m., to ensure that people could be home by 9 p.m. They should sing hymns lustily but modestly and in time and not alter them. Itinerants should be considerate to their horses. Preachers were allowed no tobacco or spirits and expected to fast regularly. They must wear plain, cheap clothes, but always be neat and clean: 'Let none ever see a ragged Methodist.' (This was an important virtue for Wesley. It was he who first said, 'Cleanliness is next to godliness,' and when he could find little good to say of his wife, he told her, 'I still love you... for your uncommon neatness and cleanliness.') Preachers should 'converse sparingly and cautiously with women' – more sparingly and cautiously, presumably, than Wesley managed to do himself – and ensure that men and women were seated separately in all meetings. Stewards must organize relief for those in need – not just send money, but where possible, take it in person. If they had to turn away any who asked, they must do it kindly: 'If you cannot relieve, do not grieve the poor.' Wesley also decreed that all preachers must be full time, so pressing was the need, and at the 1767 Conference (which was for the first time open to all Methodist preachers, rather than those hand picked by Wesley) he gave them a year's notice to quit their jobs.

By 1769, Wesley felt the time had come to legislate for his death. Having given up trying to find a single successor, he told the preachers that they should meet in London when he died and vote on a committee to oversee the Connexion, each member acting as moderator in succession. A couple of years later, he was trying to persuade John Fletcher to be his successor instead, but he never agreed.

He also, unofficially, made rules for women preachers. He told Sarah Crosby, in 1769, to preach but to avoid as far as possible the form of preaching. Thus, she should never speak from a biblical text, her 'exhortations' should be broken into four- or five-minute segments, interspersed with prayers, and she should call the meetings 'prayer meetings'. In High Wycombe in 1769, Hannah Ball started the first children's Sunday school, beating Robert Raikes, to whom the credit usually goes, by 11 years.

Wesley's relationship with his wife continued to be distant and unhappy. Arriving in Bristol just before midnight, three days before the 1768 Conference, he heard the next morning that Molly was dangerously ill in London and immediately took a carriage. Arriving at the Foundery apartment at one o'clock the following morning, he found the fever had turned, so at two o'clock turned round and headed back to Bristol.

According to an early biographer, Wesley 'believed the Lord overruled this painful business for good; and that, if Mrs Wesley had been a better wife, he might have been unfaithful to the great work to which God had called him'. Whether or not their unhappiness was the work of God, there can be little doubt how greatly it benefited the Methodist movement, keeping him on the road while Charles, a happy husband and father, was now virtually retired. As Berridge of Everton put it, 'Matrimony has quite maimed poor Charles and might have spoiled John and George [Whitefield], if a wise master had not graciously sent them a brace of ferrets.'

Wesley maintained his constant and varied flow of writings. When, in 1771, he published his *Collected Works*, they already filled 32 volumes. He was now getting a handsome income from his books, but rather than spending it on a more comfortable life, he gave away the vast majority of it – as much as £1,400 in one year – and lived, as ever, on £30. In 1768, shortly after he was bequeathed £1,000, his sister Martha asked if he could spare some of it. She was too late as it was all gone: 'Money never stays with *me*,' he explained: 'it would burn me if it did. I throw it out of my hands as soon as possible, lest it find a way into my heart.' Wesley, increasingly worried that other Methodists, unlike him, were indeed getting burnt, repeatedly admonished them not to love worldly riches:

> This will be their grand danger: as they are industrious and frugal, they must needs increase in goods. This appears already: in London, Bristol, and most other trading towns, those who are in business have increased in substance sevenfold, some of them twenty, yea, a hundredfold. What need, then, have these of the strongest warnings, lest they be entangled therein and perish?

What about Wesley's own personal faith? The undulations of his spiritual life are hidden behind the most impassive mask in almost all of Wesley's writings, yet one – a most extraordinary letter to Charles in June 1766 – stands out from the thousands. There he bares his soul in the most bleak and moving way:

> In one of my last I was saying that I do not feel the wrath of God abiding on me; nor can I believe it does. And yet (this is the mystery), I do not love God. I never did. Therefore I never believed, in the Christian sense of the word. Therefore I am only an honest heathen… And yet, to be so employed of God! and so hedged in that I can neither get forward nor backward! Surely there was never such an instance before, from the beginning of the world! If I ever have had *that faith*, it would not be so strange. But I never had any other evidence of the eternal or invisible world than I have now; and that is none at all, unless such as faintly shines from reason's glimmering ray. I have no direct witness (I do not say, that I am a child of God, but) of anything invisible or eternal.
>
> And yet I dare not preach otherwise than I do, either concerning faith, or love, or justification, or perfection. And yet I find rather an increase than a decrease of zeal for the whole work of God and every part of it. I am borne along, I know not how, that I can't stand still. I want all the world to come to what I do not know.

What a desolate spectacle, especially for such a single-minded spiritual zealot as Wesley. To be laid so terribly low by a lack of religious feeling makes him seem more human and more sympathetic than he usually manages to appear. It is pitiful to see his faith, even after all these years, still so dependent on the vicissitudes of his emotions. Is it not a shocking hypocrisy, though – if there is any truth, however exaggerated, in this confession – to have so constantly demanded from and promised to his followers, in person and from the pulpit, the degree of faith that he has constantly failed to reach? It is all very well to marvel at your being used to point the way you have not managed to go yourself, but constantly to put a burden on your disciples that you have constantly failed to lift yourself is monstrous.

A new issue that Wesley had to face in the 1760s, though he put it off until the very end, was America. A number of Methodists emigrated throughout the decade, mainly from Ireland. The preacher Philip Embury founded a society in New York, helped by the colourful Captain Webb – a one-eyed soldier who preached with his sword in his hand for added effect. Another group further south centred on Robert Strawbridge of Maryland. Wesley was not quick to involve himself – he had never sent preachers there, despite Whitefield's encouragement, maybe because his view of American mission was jaundiced by his own bad experience. Finally, though, the American Methodists convinced him that the fields were ripe and the harvesting fruitful, so at the 1769 Conference, Wesley asked for two volunteer preachers. Richard Boardman and Joseph Pilmoor were sent, with money to establish a New York meeting house. Wesley told several people that he was considering going himself. As Henry Rack said, 'One hardly dares to speculate about the results if he had.'

Fellowship across the predestinarian divide remained sincere but cool. In 1764, Wesley made an attempt to bridge it by writing a circular letter to every evangelical and Methodist minister, urging a formal agreement that they would always love, help and speak well of each other. It went out to 50 ministers, including George Whitefield, Vincent Perronet, John Fletcher, John Berridge, William Hicks and the recently ordained John Newton. Wesley reported to the 1769 Conference that a total of three had replied – a reflection not only of the fanciful nature of the exercise but of the suspicion that Wesley was held in, now intensified by the perfectionist revival. The following year, far from uniting in peace and love, they were thrown into by far the most savage conflict yet.

The leading predestinarian Methodist in England after Whitefield – who was often absent in America for long periods of time – was Lady Huntingdon, who had founded many chapels and was busy trying to get her preachers ordained. She enrolled six of them at St Edmund Hall, Oxford. They preached, most forthrightly and uninvited of course, in their home parishes in the holidays. Unluckily, one of their vicars was a St Edmund old boy. He complained to the college that they had turned a good barber into an insolent fanatic and, in 1768, all six were expelled.

In the flurry of tracts that followed, Wesley would naturally have supported the gospel underdogs, except that they quickly turned the dispute into a defence of Calvinist theology against the Arminian establishment. So, somehow the skirmish between the Methodists and the authorities turned into a war between the Wesleyans and predestinarians.

The St Edmund six were defended, most notably, by the fiery young predestinarian minister Augustus Montague Toplady, who later wrote the famous hymn, 'Rock of Ages'. Protesting his hatred of controversy, Wesley entered the ring in March 1770 with an extraordinary blow, even for him: he condensed and distorted Toplady's 134-page book *Absolute Predestination* into a 12-page tract, ending with these words:

> The sum of all is this: One in twenty (suppose) of mankind are elected; nineteen in twenty are reprobated. The elect shall be saved, do what they will; the reprobate will be damned, do what they can. Reader believe this or be damned. Witness my hand, A– T–.)

A volley of outraged enemy tracts and articles returned. 'For more than thirty years past,' complained Toplady, 'he has been endeavouring to palm on his credulous followers his pernicious doctrines with all the sophistry of a Jesuit, and the dictatorial authority of a pope.' Now this fraud had proved him a criminal worthy to be transported to America if not hanged.

Wesley did not reply: 'I do not fight with chimney-sweepers. He is too dirty a writer for me to meddle with. I should only foul my fingers.' This fastidiousness was just as well, as it is hard to see what he could have said in his defence.

Then Wesley chose this worst of all possible times to rethink his attitude to the evangelical foundational principle: justification by faith. Had they not taken a good idea too far? The question had been on his mind for a few years now, but the predestination dispute sharpened it suddenly. The predestinarians had taken the chance to attack Wesley's perfectionism and Wesley, in return, attacked their own belief that the elect cannot lose their salvation, claiming that it destroyed the incentive to slog one's way up the narrow road. In both cases, the predestinarians proved themselves enemies of holiness, Wesley felt, provoking him to stress it all the more. Grace – salvation as an unearned gift from God – was very important, but there was another side to the coin. Surely striving to do good helped sinners to receive that gift and it was essential if they were to hold on to it. So, in a sense, as James says, 'by works a man is justified, not by faith only'.

Wesley spoke to the Conference on this theme in August 1770 and the preachers agreed to preach up the value of good works. He then broadcast the revision to the enemy by publishing the Conference minutes.

Wesley's new emphasis was sensible enough in itself, but, introduced into this war zone, it was unlikely to get a fair hearing and neither did Wesley do anything to earn one. 'We have leaned too much toward Calvinism,' declared the bellicose minutes. Preachers should stress that heavenly reward depends on human faithfulness, they said. Believers must work for their everlasting life: 'We have received it as a maxim that "a man is to do nothing in order to justification [sic]". Nothing can be more false. Whoever desires to find favour with God should "cease from evil, and learn to do well",' and, 'We are every hour and every moment pleasing or displeasing to God, according to our works; according to the whole of our inward tempers and our outward behaviour.' If all this is true, what had the Methodists been arguing about these 30 years with the 'almost Christians' of the Church of England? 'I am afraid', concluded Wesley, 'about words.'

Howling outrage greeted this publication from the predestinarians. Wesley had betrayed the very heart of the gospel. What more blasphemous apostasies was he capable of? Even Huntingdon, the peace-maker, who the previous year had generously appointed Wesley's right-hand man John Fletcher as principle of her new predestinarian theological college at Trevecca, condemned him. She would go to the stake against the minutes, she said. Fletcher lost his job.

What of Whitefield? He was fortunate enough to avoid the conflict permanently, being on his 13th, and last, tour of America at the time. Wesley had seen Whitefield every so often throughout the 1760s, their meetings being friendly and rarely without a reflection on the deterioration of Whitefield's health: 1763, 'Humanly speaking, he is worn out', 1765, he 'seemed to be an old, old man, being fairly worn out in his master's service, though he has hardly seen fifty years', 1769, 'His soul appeared to be vigourous still, but his body was sinking apace; and, unless God interposes with his mighty hand, he must soon finish his bodily labours.'

This time, the mighty hand did not interpose, and Whitefield went to his rest on 30 September 1770 in Newbury Port, Massachusetts. He had, according to Toplady, preached 18,000 sermons. Wesley was asked to preach a memorial sermon at Whitefield's three London chapels in November – the will of the deceased cutting across the grain of the current mood. Wesley's sermon was full of love and praise and appealed for peace, but when it came to outlining Whitefield's teaching, he made no mention of his treasured doctrine of election, beyond saying, 'There are many doctrines of a less essential nature, with regard to which even the sincere children of God... are and have been divided for many ages. In these we may think and let think; we may "agree to disagree".'

To be fair, it is not easy to see what else Wesley could have done as there was no way he could have summarized predestinarian belief without condemning it and this was hardly the occasion for robust dogmatic jousting. However, the predestinarians were more furious than ever. Whitefield had been censored in death. So, the conflict reached an even greater pitch of intensity, at which it remained for years. Wesley did not write a great deal of it, rather, Fletcher took the lead, in a relatively calm and scholarly fashion. Toplady and his allies replied with all the hysterical venom that a defence of the grace of God calls for. Free-will theology, Toplady warned, 'ascends, on the ladder of blasphemy, to the mountain top of atheism'. Of Wesley himself, he said, 'I believe him to be the most rancourous hater of the gospel system that ever appeared in England.'

In 1771, Huntingdon managed to negotiate a peace. She took a team to the Wesleyan Conference and demanded that they recant the teaching of the 1770 minutes. A compromise was agreed – Wesley and 53 of his preachers signing a statement that the wording of the minutes had been unfortunate and we are indeed justified by faith not works, though not by a faith that is without works. It proved a brief truce, however, because Wesley almost immediately afterwards printed an earlier writing of Fletcher's, defending the original minutes.

The fighting did not cool much before Toplady's death in 1778. Neither side, of course, had any success in convincing the other. Apart from becoming more entrenched in their own prejudices, the only thing the hostilities achieved was to discredit Methodism as a whole in the eyes of the watching world.

CHAPTER 22

GOING TO AMERICA
(1771–80)

'And publish abroad His wonderful Name'

From 'Ye servants of God, your master proclaim'

In 1771, Molly announced that she was leaving John again. On 23 January, the *Journal* reports, 'For what cause I know not to this day, [my wife] set out for Newcastle, purposing "never to return". I did not leave her: I did not send her away: I will not call her back.'

However, just as it had proved impossible for Molly to follow John on all his travels, there were few towns in the country where she could avoid him for long – certainly not Newcastle, where she went to live with her daughter. He went there in June 1772, and they were joyfully reunited. He found her miraculously different in temperament, more wonderfully changed, he said, than anyone he had ever known. 'She is now "one full of graces, honey quite unmixed". Finding fault with nobody, but well pleased with every person and thing!'

A significant shift was also happening in Wesley's attitude to women preachers. Sarah Crosby continued her unofficial 'exhorting' and a number of other women were doing the same – the most successful being Mary Bosanquet, who had founded an orphanage in Yorkshire where Sarah was now based. However, they increasingly failed to disguise the fact that they were preaching and, in 1771, several of the male preachers started to complain.

Mary wrote to Wesley in May, humbly but compellingly claiming the full right to preach. She agreed that preaching was ordinarily the preserve of men, but pointed out that the Bible showed many examples of individual women being raised up by God. Now that she had the same 'extraordinary call' to 'act in an extraordinary manner', how could she decline it?

This was the same argument that had convinced Wesley to allow lay preaching – a risky approach that might have scared him with the prospect of women becoming as common in the pulpit as laymen. As it turned out, he was completely convinced by Mary's argument. Even Paul, he noted, while emphatically banning women's preaching in general, allowed it in Corinth, so the prohibition cannot have been absolute. Her case appealed to his powerful sense that the call of God, known in inward feelings and outward success, overshadows other considerations. Although there was no change yet to the official rules of the Connexion, Mary and Sarah were allowed to preach on the same basis as any man, and Sarah also took to the road. She travelled nearly 1,000 miles a year, speaking at over 200 public meetings and 600 class or band meetings.

In 1771, a local revival broke out in Weardale, in Durham. Again, it revived the charismatic phenomena of the early days of Methodism, although Wesley was pleased to report that there were fewer visions and more conversions than in the Everton revival. Such events were becoming a recurrent feature of Methodism, perhaps because they allowed believers to recapture both the excitement and the passionate commitment of the early days of their faith, as well as drawing in new believers and backsliders. The revival was a sign of the times in another way too: children and young people played prominent parts, experiencing charismatic manifestations, undergoing evangelical conversions and evangelizing. Such things had happened in Ireland in 1758 and a number of times in Kingswood school, and now became a recurrent feature of local revivals. This was presumably because the evangelical emphasis on personal conversion excluded infants, unlike the collective religion of traditional Anglicanism, and now that so many children of Methodists were coming of age, a moment of personal crisis seemed necessary to turn them from the children of Christians into Christian children.

In July 1773, Wesley preached to his largest audience ever, at Gwennap Pit in Cornwall – 32,000 by his reckoning. 'Perhaps the first time that a man of seventy had been heard by thirty thousand persons at once!'

A second pair of preachers went to America in 1771 (Wesley always sent them in pairs, as Jesus had sent the apostles). One was the great 26-year-old preacher Francis Asbury, the 'Wesley of America'. In 1773, the senior preacher Thomas Rankin was sent to take the reins and led the first American Conference, imposing Wesleyan rules as well he could. However, America was not Britain and the same level of discipline proved impossible there. The Church of England did not have the same hegemony as at home – 'There is no church that is established more than another,' as Pilmoor put it, so Methodists saw less reason than ever to defer to it. Hence, Strawbridge insisted on administering the sacraments and Wesley had to turn a blind eye. This lack of control also allowed Robert Williams in Virginia to become the only preacher in the Connexion to publish without Wesley's censorship.

American Methodism grew quickly. In 1771 there were 316 members; the 1773 Conference counted 1,160; the following year there were 2,000. It also spread elsewhere in the Americas. In 1773 – the year of the Boston Tea Party – the first Methodists went north into Canada, worried by the worsening political situation. In the Caribbean, the Antiguan landowner Nathaniel Gilbert had started preaching in 1759 to both blacks and whites. By 1773, Gilbert had 60 society members in Antigua, two-thirds of whom were black; when he died the following year there were 200. Under his successor, John Baxter, the society soon grew to 1,100, eight of whom were white.

Wesleyan attitudes to slavery make for an interesting comparison with Whitefield's. Whitefield owned 25 slaves after having been instrumental in overturning the late Governor Oglethorpe's ban on slavery in Georgia. He was convinced that only black labour, designed to withstand the heat of the deep-southern day, would restore the fortunes of his orphan house and the colony as a whole. 'I trust many of them will be brought to Jesus,' he said. He had seen the conversion of owners transform the treatment of slaves and, indeed, proved to be a model and well-loved slave owner himself, providing his slaves with what was just and equal, knowing that he also had a master in heaven. So he made his contribution to the survival of slavery in America and added his name to the interminable list of those who have used the name of Jesus to justify the most blatant and shameful evil.

Wesley, not having the same investment in America, was able to see the issue in starker terms. In 1772, after reading the anti-slavery work of the Quaker Anthony Benezet, he denounced slavery as 'that execrable sum of all villainies', regurgitating the book later in his *Thoughts on Slavery*: 'Did the Creator intend that the noblest creatures in the visible world should live such a life as this?... I absolutely deny all slave-holding to be consistent with any degree of natural justice.' In 1784, the Wesleyan Connexion in America threatened to expel slave owners, though it backed down. Most remarkable of all, the Antiguan society – between the death of its founder Nathaniel Gilbert and the arrival of his official replacement – revived the spirit of the early Church, being run for several years very successfully by female slave preachers.

When the American war broke out at Lexington and Concord in April 1775, Wesley was surprisingly sympathetic to the rebels. He rather surprised himself, in fact, as he said in a letter of unsolicited advice to the Secretary of State for the Colonies, Lord Dartmouth:

> All my prejudices are against the Americans. For I am an High Churchman, the son of an High Churchman, bred up from my childhood in the highest notions of passive obedience and non-resistance. And yet, in spite of all my rooted prejudice, I cannot avoid thinking (if I think at all) that an oppressed people asked for nothing more than their legal rights, and that in the most modest and inoffensive manner which the nature of the thing would allow.

Not only justice but common sense warned against the war, he argued. The Americans had all the advantages and our European neighbours were bound to attack while all our soldiers were 'cutting the throats of their brethren in America'. A greater danger still was from British rebels. Wesley claimed, not unreasonably, to speak with a greater cross-section of the populace than any other person and warned that the revolution of the 1640s was poised to repeat itself: the people are 'just ripe for open rebellion... They want nothing but a leader.' The judgment of God on 'the astonishing *luxury* of the rich and the *profaneness* of rich and poor' was ready to strike.

A few months later, Wesley's attitude to the war was entirely reversed by Samuel Johnson. The two great men had become friends and enjoyed chatting when Wesley could spare the time, which was not often: 'I hate to meet John Wesley,' complained Johnson; 'the dog enchants you with his conversation, and then breaks away to go and visit some old woman.' One would not have expected Methodist preaching to appeal to Johnson's sense of propriety, but he applauded their selfless labour and attributed their success 'to their expressing themselves in a plain and familiar manner, which is the only way to do good to the common people'. Johnson now poured his prejudice against the American brethren – whom he had always considered 'a race of convicts, [who] ought to be thankful for any thing we allow them short of hanging' – into a pamphlet entitled *Taxation No Tyranny*. Britain had founded, provided for and protected its colonies, he argued, and now that the occupants had grown rich there they wanted to keep them. Americans had forfeited the vote by leaving their home, but still owed tax as they were on British soil. They called for liberty, but already had as much as most English people and, anyway, 'How is it that we hear the loudest *yelps* for liberty among the drivers of negroes?' Wesley read it, fell for it and plagiarized it. He edited it into a pamphlet entitled *A Calm Address to the American Colonies* and published it under his own name.

Wesley was a serial plagiarist and simply saw nothing wrong with regurgitating other people's work. As a writer, he inserted other people's writings into his own as happily and as unannounced as he inserted his own into other people's as an editor. He had always done it, apparently believing that good reading was worth repeating and that if he agreed with others' opinions they were his own and should be broadcast as such, giving them a wider readership, at least among Methodists.

This time, however, he was in trouble. Johnson himself graciously told Wesley that he appreciated the complement, but others were less

generous and publicly decried his disgraceful fraud – especially, with
depressing predictability, enemy Methodists. Toplady gleefully
trumpeted Wesley's intellectual bankruptcy in *The Old Fox Tarr'd and
Feather'd*, and again Fletcher came to Wesley's defence. Wesley's only
response was to reprint the tract with an acknowledgment to Johnson.

His private life also had its troubles: the entente with his wife was
over. In March 1774, she wrote him her one surviving letter, full of
complaints about her persecution by his acolytes: 'My dear friend, let
me beg of you for God's sake, for your own sake, put a stop to this
torrrent of evil that is poured out against me.' He wrote her a long
letter in July, retracing the whole of their sorry relationship in a final
attempt to change her heart. He listed her multitudinous crimes and
failings, her theft and lies, her quarrelling and stubbornness, her
murdering his character to vindicate her own (and 'of what importance
is *your* character to mankind?') – all this despite the 'unspeakable
blessing that you have a husband who knows your temper and can bear
with it'. As ever, he scorned the notion of compromise and the nearest
he came to admitting any fault on his part was when he explained that
the list of her faults was incomplete because he did not have his journal
to hand: 'I have therefore only my memory to depend on; and that is
not very retentive of evil.' The truth is, I think, that neither was guilty
of any great crime against the other, beyond the folly of agreeing to
marry in the first place. It was, as the lay preacher Hampson said, a
'preposterous union' as John's punishing lifestyle and female
friendships would have defeated all but the hardiest and meekest of
women and Molly was neither. After 1776, there is no record of their
meeting.

Wesley's revision of his evangelical theology continued, proving that
the 1770 Conference minutes had not been a momentary aberration.
The Holy Club years – which on his conversion he had written off as a
futile attempt to save himself without the only thing that mattered,
faith – he now looked back on with septuagenarian nostalgia. He told
his brother:

> I often cry out, 'Give me back my former life.' Let me be again an
> Oxford Methodist! I am often in doubt whether it would not be

best for me to resume all my Oxford rules, great and small. I did then walk closely with God and redeem the time. But what have I been doing these thirty years?

When in 1775, he reissued his *Journal* from 1735 as part of his *Collected Works*, it contained some startling revisions. The evangelical evaluation of his state of damnation on returning from Georgia in 1738, which he wrote up after his conversion, now had some footnotes. For example, 'I who went to America to convert others, was never myself converted to God. [I am not sure of this.]' 'I am "a child of wrath". [I believe not.]' His May 1738 survey of his life said of the Holy Club days, 'By my continued endeavour to keep his whole law, inward and outward, to the utmost of my power, I was persuaded that I should be accepted of him, and that I was in a state of salvation.' He now added, 'And I believe I was.' In 1779, he mentioned that 'The present revival of religion in England has already continued fifty years,' thus dating it to the founding of the Holy Club rather than the start of the evangelical movement.

Another reminder of the Holy Club days was his former pupil Richard Morgan, whom Wesley had met up with again in Ireland in 1769. In 1775, he paid him another visit and found the Morgans' only child on her deathbed. Distressed not so much by her illness as by her manners, Wesley afterwards wrote the last in his series of appallingly unkind letters to the Morgan family. This is Wesley at his very worst. The girl, he told Richard, was the most spoiled he had ever seen and he had ruined her good nature and breeding. Her illness was no excuse, as 'pain should soften, not roughen our temper'. 'I know not what she is fit for.' If she lived to marry she would be a torment to her husband. 'Happy would it be [for] both her and you if God would speedily take her to himself!' He opened the letter by promising it was 'one of the greatest... instances of friendship', and closed by warning that if Richard showed it to Mrs Morgan he would never speak to him again.

In 1776, as war raged in Massachusetts and New York and the Americans declared independence, Wesley continued his anti-American pamphlets and his preachers continued to leave America. With this kind of PR, it is not surprising that Methodist membership in the northern circuits halved in two years. More surprising was that membership in America as a whole shot up, thanks to a great revival in Virginia led by Rankin and the evangelical minister Devereux Jarratt. Visited by the same convulsions and anguished cries for mercy that accompanied Wesley's early preaching, it was, according to Jarratt, 'a revival of religion as great as was perhaps ever known, in country places, in so short a time'. In the two years from 1775 to 1777, Methodist numbers in Virginia rose from 955 to 4,379, accounting for about half the Methodists in America.

At home, two of the great monuments of Wesley's Methodism were established. The first was the City Road Chapel in London, which Wesley opened on 1 November 1778. A large, impressive church building, though without a hint of ostentation, it had room for 2,000, according to Wesley's typically generous estimate, with a new house designed to sleep Wesley and four other preachers next door. It created more problems in the troubled relationship between Methodists and the Church. There was a campaign to have meetings there at the same time as church services, though Wesley quashed it. The chapel also increased tensions between the pro-Church clergy – especially Charles – who succeeded in monopolizing the pulpit and the itinerant preachers – including the recently returned Rankin – who despaired of Charles's 'dry and lifeless' preaching.

The other great monument was *Hymns for the Use of Methodists*, which Wesley published in 1780. He compiled the best of the many Methodist hymn books into one volume, 'not so large as to be either cumbersome, or expensive: and... large enough to contain such a weight of hymns as will not soon be worn threadbare'. It was a definitive distillation of Wesleyan theology and spirituality and, according to the philosopher James Martineau, 'the grandest instrument of popular religious culture that Christendom has ever produced'.

CHAPTER 23

PARTINGS
(1780–91)

'Bold I approach the eternal Throne'
From 'And can it be'

Three intertangled issues dominated the last decade of Wesley's life: America, what was to become of Methodism after his death and, above all, separation from the Church of England. While UK membership had risen healthily throughout the 1770s from around 30,000 to 43,830 at the time of 1780 Conference, the number in America had grown from a couple of hundred to 10,139. Yet all those American Methodists had no ordained minister and Francis Asbury was, by 1778, the only one of Wesley's apostles who refused to return from the United States, explaining that it was not 'the part of a good shepherd to leave the flock in time of danger'. Throughout the war, he travelled across the States, through trackless forest, river and bog, preaching amid fighting and anarchy.

His reward was to be invited by the 1779 Conference of Northern States to become General Superintendent, but the need for other preachers and ministers was obviously desperate. The only thing that prevented the Americans ordaining their own ministers was Wesleyan loyalty to the Church of England, but with America at war with England this loyalty made less sense than ever. The Southerners, in fact, decided to ordain and were only persuaded to put the plan on hold when the northern Conference (after much arm-twisting from Asbury) threatened to disown them. Thus, the intolerable dearth of sacraments continued and Asbury started to petition Wesley to allow his lay preachers to administer them.

Still not ready for this resort, Wesley himself petitioned the Church hierarchy to ordain some of his men as ministers for America, but without success, despite the fact that the Anglican church in the States was itself facing the same crisis. The Bishop of London refused one of his requests on the basis that 'There are three ministers in that country already,' then went on, according to Wesley, to ordain other men who, in contrast to his own unscholarly candidate, 'knew something of Greek and Latin, but who knew no more of saving souls than of catching whales'. Wesley's options were narrowing.

As Wesley's last decade passed, many of his fellow runners beat him to the finishing line. The first was his wife, who died on 8 October 1781. John did not attend her funeral and the one item of her £5,000 estate that she left to him was a ring. This seems fair enough, though, as she had a daughter to provide for and anything she gave her husband would have gone straight to the poor.

He approached his 80th birthday as vigorous as ever, still marvelling at and expounding on his unimpaired fitness and still constantly touring the British Isles – 'Repose is not for me in this world' – although he now took a chaise more frequently and rode less. The preacher John Hampson described him as sprightly and muscular:

> A narrow, plaited stock, a coat with a small upright collar, no
> buckles at the knees, no silk or velvet in any part of his apparel,
> and a head as white as snow, gave the idea of something primitive
> and apostolical; while an air of neatness and cleanliness was
> diffused over his whole person.

Nearly half a century had transformed him from a nationwide scandal into almost a national treasure. Fear and hatred had widely mellowed into veneration and he was often asked to preach in the same churches that had once turned him away: 'The tide is turned,' he said in January 1783, 'and I have more invitations to preach in churches than I can accept.'

One of his recurrent worries in these changing times was the wealth of Methodists. Over the decades, Methodist values had prospered the faithful. This is because Wesley taught them the virtues of industry and abstinence and his religion encouraged literacy, as well as articulate self-confidence, while discouraging spending on spirits and tobacco, jewellery and ribbons, gambling and the theatre. Wesley lamented that there was a self-destructive streak to 'true Christianity': holiness accumulates wealth, which destroys the soul and thus the faith is its own undoing. For 40 years he had reiterated the maxim by which he himself lived – 'Earn all you can; save all you can; give all you can' – but it seems that his followers found the third point, which was the whole purpose of the exercise, harder to remember than the other two or at least took it less literally than Wesley himself. Hence, his three-point approach to money was a major theme of his sermons now, with the last point ever more boldly emphasized.

Just as separation from the Church of England was coming to seem inevitable, news came that Lady Huntingdon's Connexion had gone ahead of them. Over the years, she had built meeting houses around the south of England, shielded ever more precariously behind her aristocratic right to have private chapels. However, when she converted a theatre in Clerkenwell in 1777, she met her comeuppance. The parish priest sued her preachers for encroaching on his monopoly and, in 1782, she was forced to register the place as a Dissenting chapel to avoid closure. The following year, two ordained ministers in her Connexion quit the Church of England, with her blessing, and ordained her preachers.

The ministers' defence for their actions was that the New Testament knows only one order of priesthood, so the traditional distinction between ordinary presbyter/priest and bishop is not binding and every minister has as much right to ordain as a bishop. In fact, Wesley had been propounding this theory himself for some years, but it was Huntingdon who was first forced to put it into practice and so founded a new denomination.

As the American war came to an end in 1783, Asbury continued to complain to Wesley on behalf of the deprived American flock. There were now thousands of children who had not been baptized and many adults who had gone years without Holy Communion. Wesley had to act or face his own American revolt. The question was how best to balance the need for ministers with the danger of inflaming anti-Methodist opinion. In the meantime, he officially appointed Asbury as

General Assistant for America, a measure evidently intended to affirm Asbury's authority while keeping it subordinate to Wesley's own, as well as playing for time.

The year 1784 was a momentous one, as it was the year Wesley settled both the American question and the Methodist succession. The problem with the latter was that Wesley, now 80, *was* Methodism: he not only ruled his Connexion, but legally owned its assets. The Conference of preachers had no legal existence. So, in February 1784, Wesley drew up the Deed of Declaration, establishing the Conference as the ruling body of the Wesleyan Connexion, transferring all his authority to it on his and Charles's deaths. The deed required annual meetings, establishing the posts of president and secretary to be re-elected every three years. The most strongly contested part of the deed was that membership of the Conference was restricted to 100 preachers (there were currently 191) and, moreover, that Wesley named them, passing over some senior figures in favour of those he considered more able, loyal or orthodox. Some of the excluded 91 quit the Connexion in protest, including the American missionary Pilmoor and Wesley's biographer-to-be Hampson. Nevertheless, the continuation and stability of Wesley's Connexion was assured and, in the absence of an heir, it was transformed from an autocracy to an aristocracy. However, as Wesley made very plain, nothing was to change as long as he was alive: 'No power that I have enjoyed is given up.'

As for America, Wesley's decision was to ordain ministers himself. Priest and bishop being 'the same order', he argued, he had the power and the right. He was 'as much a Christian bishop as the Archbishop of Canterbury', he said. Fletcher tried to dissuade him and Charles begged him to at least wait until he was dead, but Wesley saw no alternative, so, at the July/August Conference, he asked for volunteers. Two lay preachers were chosen – Richard Whatcoat and Thomas Vasey – and, on 1 September, Wesley – along with two evangelical ministers, Thomas Coke and James Creighton – laid hands on them, ordaining them deacons and, the following day, priests. As if this was not scandalous enough, he then 'ordained' Coke and made him bishop for America.

What exactly Wesley meant by this latter rite is open to debate. Although Wesley called it an 'ordination', it is unthinkable that he considered Coke's Anglican ordination invalid and was re-ordaining him a Methodist minister. Presumably, therefore, he was consecrating him as bishop or 'superintendent'. Wesley used the latter term rather than 'bishop' in the official document, but this is simply a literal translation of the New Testament word for 'bishop', *episcopos*, evidently chosen because it would cause less offence than 'bishop' and evoke a more 'primitive', biblical idea of the episcopal office. Coke understood the rite to confer on him 'the power of ordaining others', but as the whole basis of Wesley's right to ordain was that he had that power as a minister of the Church of England, this seems somewhat self-contradictory. However, it was certainly not Wesley's intention to give the go-ahead for all Methodist ministers to ordain as they felt led, so it seems (to impose order on some rather confused claims) that Coke's 'ordination' was intended to give him extraordinary authority to exercise that power that all ministers have in potential.

Wesley now had to explain and defend his actions. He stressed not only his right to ordain and the desperate need in America, but also the freedom that American independence had given him. There was now no state church there, so 'I violate no order and invade no man's right by appointing and sending labourers into the harvest.' Also, the official document stressed that Wesley was acting to fulfil the Americans' wishes to 'adhere to the doctrines and discipline of the Church of England'. One of his most irreconcilable critics was Charles, who only heard about the ordinations afterwards on the Methodist grapevine and, among other protests, attacked his brother in a published poem:

> So easily are Bishops made
> By men's or women's whim?
> Wesley his hands on Coke hath laid,
> But who laid hands on him?

The irrelevant mention of women recalls John's use of women preachers and hints that his lawless egalitarianism may have had even more sinister extremes to reach yet.

One might as well be hung for a sheep as a goat, so Wesley took the opportunity of these ordinations to rewrite the Book of Common Prayer for the Americans. The result, *The Sunday Service of the Methodists in North America*, provides a wide window into Wesley's mature spirituality. He deliberately made the service shorter – an uncharacteristic concession to human weakness. He toned down claims for the regenerative power of baptism, replaced the terms 'priest' and 'bishop' with 'elder' and 'superintendent' and made no requirement to kneel for Communion, though he personally was in favour of doing so. He removed rites for holy days and the Church calendar. There was no service of confirmation (being unbiblical) or visitation of the sick (a duty not requiring liturgy). He bowdlerized the Psalms, finding the honesty of biblical worship 'highly improper for the mouths of a Christian congregation' and dropped the Athanasian creed with its overconfident damnations. He left out 15 of the Thirty-Nine Articles, extensively abridging the remainder. The missing articles included 'Christ Alone Without Sin', which denied perfection, 'Predestination and Election', for obvious reasons, and most notably 'Works Before Justification', which, with its overstatement of the contrast between before and after justification, was maybe too much like hard-line evangelicalism for Wesley's mature tastes.

Wesley's new clergy set off for the United States on 18 September 1784. It remained to be seen how Asbury would take this new arrangement. The plan was for Coke to ordain him as fellow superintendent, but when they met up in Delaware in November, Asbury insisted that such appointments needed to be approved by the American Conference. This was a shrewd move that endeared him all the more to the flock, strengthening the American Methodists' sense of independence from the home Church, while also ensuring that his own authority stood independently of that of Coke and even Wesley.

Coke was forced to agree and the Conference met on Christmas Eve 1784, after Asbury had sent Coke on a lightning 900-mile tour of the States. The Conference unanimously approved the scheme and Asbury was appointed superintendent. The Americans affirmed their loyalty to Wesley and their adherence to his theology, but on their own terms. Asbury described their relationship with the home Church as 'Union but no subordination; connexion but no subjection'. The Conference also considered an offer of union from the newly independent Anglicans of America, but this came to nothing.

Even after these ordinations, Wesley continued to insist that Methodists were full members of the Church of England. America was a special case and in England they would continue to be subject to Anglican order. He continued to declare, 'When the Methodists leave the Church, God will leave them' and 'To lose a thousand, yea ten thousand, of our people would be a less evil than this.' However, this stance became ever more difficult to maintain during his remaining years and his declarations on this point increasingly lacked dogmatism.

Less than a year after the American ordinations, Wesley ordained three ministers for Scotland. Here there was an established Church of course, unlike America, but as it was Presbyterian, Wesley could still deny parting from the Church of England. The awkwardness of this situation is exemplified by the way he insisted that the Scottish ministers take off their vestments before entering England. In 1788, however, he ordained Alexander Mather as a minister (and probably superintendent) for England in what looks like a passing of the mantle, so the pretence that Methodism did not have its own separate clergy was finally impossible to maintain.

The only practical difference left between Methodists and the Dissenters now was that the Methodists attended their parish churches as well as their own meetings. However, even this was unpopular and Wesley had increasing difficulty enforcing it. The members of the Deptford society were especially importunate that their meeting time be pushed back to the same time as church service: 'This would be a formal separation from the Church,' replied Wesley, preventing even those who wanted from attending both and, therefore, 'totally unlawful for me to do'. On his next visit, however, in 1787, he found them 'a den of lions', the leaders 'mad for leaving the Church'. Reasoning failed and only threats won him this round: 'If you are resolved you may have your meeting in church hours; but, remember, from that time you will see my face no more.'

However, already by that year's Conference he was making rules to allow Methodist meetings to clash with morning prayer in certain circumstances – where the parish priest was wicked or a heretic or where there were too few churches in the area, for example. In 1788, he allowed meetings at the same time as the churches as long as they never clashed with a Communion service. His explanation for these concessions – 'not to *prepare for* but to *prevent* a separation from the Church' – sums up his attitude to the whole issue.

Wesley ended up arguing that Methodists were still church men and women merely because they had not declared the 'total and immediate separation' that Huntingdon had when they 'agreed to form themselves into a separate body without delay, to go to church no more, and to have no more connection with the Church of England than with the Church of Rome'. The claim that Methodists cannot have separated because they never announced such intentions is a measure of how little was left of the strands that tied Methodism to the Church.

The American Methodists were at the same time getting used to their new relationship with their mother Church – one that, as they saw it, balanced unity with independence. This was a concept that Wesley himself never really grasped. He decreed a Conference in Baltimore in 1787, for example, to appoint Whatcoat as superintendent, but the Americans had prior arrangements and did not approve of Wesley's choice anyway, so they ignored him. They acknowledged themselves his 'sons in the gospel', but, said Asbury, 'for our old Daddy to appoint Conferences when and where he pleased, to appoint a joint superintendent with me, were strokes of power we did not understand'.

When Asbury and Coke started calling themselves 'bishops' and founded 'Cokesbury College', Wesley was aghast at their presumption:

> I study to be little: you study to be great. I creep: you strut along. I found a school: you a college! Nay, and call it after your own names! O beware, do not seek to be something!...
>
> How can you, how dare you suffer yourself to be called Bishop? I shudder, I start at the very thought! Men may call me a knave or a fool, a rascal, a scoundrel, and I am content; but they shall never by my consent call me Bishop! For my sake, for God's sake, for Christ's sake put a full end to this!

It was the last letter Asbury received from Wesley and he was hurt, but his only response was to praise the Lord for such soul-building trials. That same year, the American Methodists officially named themselves the Methodist Episcopal Church of America.

By 1790, membership in the United States was 61,811 – almost six times what it had been at the start of the previous decade. Over 40,000 of those had come in the last four years, demonstrating how much good independence and peace had done them. This did not yet quite overtake numbers in the United Kingdom, which, in the same time, had added 27,633 to give them 71,463.

Wesley's relationships with women continued to be of interest in his old age. A larger circle of pious young women than ever had the benefit of his exhortations, enquiries into their thoughts and feelings and tender protestations of concern and affection. He always tried to dissuade them from marriage – the class leader Nancy Bolton was saved from three suitors by his intervention and only married after his death. The unflattering impression this gives of a possessiveness that finds romantic fulfilment in keeping a young evangelical harem unattached may not be entirely undeserved. Yet Wesley strove to keep his male preachers unattached too, and even if this anti-marriage policy was unduly influenced by his own sour experience, its equal application to men and women for the sake of their service reflects an appreciation of women's abilities that had not so far been one of Protestant Christianity's greatest strengths.

A small number of women preachers continued to play a significant role in Wesley's Connexion. Admittedly, he wrote to John Peacock of Grimsby demanding 'a final stop to the preaching of women in this circuit', yet in other places he continued to support it. The preacher Mary Bosanquet married Wesley's close friend and defender John Fletcher in 1781 and the couple operated virtually as joint ministers in his Madeley parish. In 1787, Wesley went further than ever and officially recognized Sarah Mallet as preacher for Norwich.

John Fletcher died in 1785 and received a great eulogy from Wesley at his funeral. Another old friend, Vincent Perronet, the minister who advised him in his courtship with Grace and Molly (with no very great success, admittedly) died the same year. The one old soulmate who was still with John was his brother Charles. Though their relationship had long been chequered, often strained and sometimes stormy, there was an unbreakable bond between them. John was close to his three children, especially Sally, offering them instruction on everything from the spiritual life to the new fad of sea bathing. The two boys were becoming celebrated musicians and Uncle John enjoyed their concerts, though he preferred simple hymn singing and did not enjoy the extremely grand company that attended them. He worried much about the state of the brothers' souls – all the more so when Samuel became a Catholic and refused to hear Methodist preaching.

On 29 March 1788, Charles died at home in Marylebone. John was not present, nor did he make it to the funeral, the news reaching him in Macclesfield only the previous day. John, true to his belief, did not 'grieve as those without hope', but three weeks after Charles's death, he came to lead a service in Bolton. In one of the most elegant buildings with one of the most ardent memberships in the country, Wesley reflected. The most angelic choir of almost 100 children sang the first hymn. The second hymn was Charles's great poem, 'Wrestling Jacob'. John read out the opening lines, '… My company before is gone / And I am left alone with thee,' sat down, put his head in his hands and cried.

Wesley still continued the *Journal*'s reports on his own health and, even in his eighties, they did not become more negative, merely more frequent. On his 82nd birthday, he declared, 'It is now eleven years since I have felt any such thing as weariness… I dare not impute this to natural causes: it is the will of God.' His only illnesses were those inflicted by his own actions. That winter he had caught a fever trudging all day through London streets ankle deep in melting snow begging £200 so that he could add clothes to his annual provision of food and fuel for the poor.

At 84, he found that the only effects of age were that he was slower at walking uphill, at reading by candlelight, and at remembering. On his 85th birthday, he had to add that he could now barely see out of his left eye (though he found no other defects in his senses) and felt pains in his right eye, right temple, right shoulder and right arm, though never violent nor for long. Still, however, he travelled and preached without the least weariness and felt no 'decay in writing sermons which I do as readily, and I believe as correctly, as ever'. He attributed this wonderful strength to 'the power of God, fitting me for the work to which I am called' and 'to the prayers of his children', as well as, more practically, constant exercise and travel, a carefree life and always sleeping well, rising at four and preaching at five.

After all these upbeat assessments, his entry for New Year's Day, 1790, comes as a shock:

> I am now an old man, decayed from head to foot. My eyes are
> dim; my right hand shakes much; my mouth is hot and dry every
> morning; I have a lingering fever almost every day; my motion
> is weak and slow. However, blessed be God, I do not slack my
> labour: I can preach and write still.

On 28 June, his 87th birthday, he reviewed the decline over the last year:

> My eyes were so dim that no glasses would help me. My strength
> likewise quite forsook me and probably will not return in this
> world. But I feel no pain from head, to foot; only it seems nature
> is exhausted and, humanly speaking, will sink more and more, till
> 'The weary springs of life stand still at last.'

Even now he continued his preaching tours and other duties quite relentlessly. In 1790, he covered London, Bristol, the Isle of Wight, the Midlands, Lincolnshire, the North West, Yorkshire, Newcastle and Scotland. In Falmouth, where he had suffered one of his most frightening mob attacks in 1745, 'high and low lined the streets, from one end of the town to the other, out of stark love and kindness, gaping and staring as if the king were going by'. In Norwich, where bad feeling had lingered for many years, he preached to an overflowing house: 'How wonderfully is the tide turned! I am become an honourable man at Norwich.'

Wesley preached his last outdoor sermon under a tree in Winchelsea in October 1790. After his death, the tree was cut down and relics in the form of wood and leaves have been kept to this day. By 1791, Wesley was confined to London with occasional trips to the villages. On Thursday 17 April, Wesley took ill in Lambeth, but recovered enough to preach three times the following week.

Wesley's last sermon was in Leatherhead on Wednesday 23 April: 'Seek ye the Lord while he may be found'. On the journey to and from there, he read the autobiography of the African slave Gustavus Vassa, which he had helped to finance. Inspired by it, he dictated his justly celebrated last letter to his young friend and admirer William Wilberforce, who was preparing for the 1791 abolition debate. Wesley was not a reformer – his answer to social injustice was either local organization or the pen – but he gave his blessing to the man who, in many ways, took his mantle:

Dear Sir,
Unless the divine power has raised you up to be as Athanasius against the world, I see not how you can go through your glorious enterprise in opposing that execrable villainy, which is the scandal of religion, of England, and of human nature. Unless God has raised you up for this very thing, you will be worn out by the opposition of men and devils. But if God be for you, who can be against you? Are all of them together stronger than God? O be not weary of well doing. Go on, in the name of God and in the power of his might, till even American slavery (the vilest that ever saw the sun) shall vanish away before it.

Reading this morning a tract wrote by a poor African, I was particularly struck by that circumstance, that a man who has a black skin, being wronged or outraged by a white man, can have no redress; it being a *law* in all our Colonies that the *oath* of a black against a white goes for nothing. What villainy is this!

That he who has guided you from youth up may continue to strengthen you in this and all things is the prayer of, dear sir,
Your affectionate servant,
John Wesley

Back at City Road, Wesley fell ill again and grew increasingly weak until he could barely speak. On Tuesday 1 March, he called for pen and ink, but could not write. His devoted bandleader Betsy Ritchie said:

'Let me write for you, sir; tell me what you would say.'
'Nothing,' answered Wesley, 'but that God is with us.'

He then astonished his attendants by bursting out with the last hymn he had led at the City Road a week before:

I'll praise my Maker while I've breath,
   And when my voice is lost in death
Praise shall employ my nobler pow'rs;
   My days of praise shall ne'er be past,
While life, and thought, and being last,
     Or immortality endures.

He urged that his sermon on the love of God be printed and given away for free, but then his mumbling became incomprehensible, so he merely repeated at intervals, 'The best of all is God is with us!' Throughout the night he tried to sing the same hymn, but could only get out, 'I'll praise...', 'I'll praise...'. After a last 'Farewell', he died on Wednesday morning.

The funeral was scheduled for the following Wednesday, Wesley of course requesting the simplest of rites. By the Tuesday night, so many thousands had gathered that the inner circle secretly brought the burial forward to 5 a.m. (Wesley would never have wanted to lie in any later), but still they did not beat the crowds.

CHAPTER 24

THE LONG RUN

'Thousand thousand Saints attending'
From 'Lo! He comes with clouds descending'

> Six lives of Wesley have already been published… What
> then justifies the present writer in publishing another?
>
> Luke Tyerman, Life and Times of John Wesley, *1871*

I suppose any really fascinating person is likely to be a web of
contradictions and certainly that is the case with Wesley. The most
obvious of these by now will be his undying devotion to the Church of
England, while founding its most successful rival denomination. He felt
a filial loyalty to the Church, which he tried to instil in his followers,
but committed as he was above all to spiritual revival, he had to claim
the same freedom from ecclesiastical restrictions that Dissenters
enjoyed. He relentlessly challenged the complacency and convention
of the establishment and championed that most disruptive of religious
phenomena, charismatic gifts, yet all the time abhorring disorder and
innovation.

Similarly with politics. He was enough of a proto-capitalist to urge
Methodists – most successfully – to climb the earnings ladder by means
of graft and thrift, but in the same breath would advocate – as he
practised – the voluntary redistribution of all but the most basic wealth.
He was an authoritarian egalitarian, though in the opposite way to
totalitarian communists, preaching social order while subverting it in
practice. He believed profoundly in rank, but despised the monied

classes, loving the poor not out of charitable condescension but genuine fellow feeling – despite in later years making an extremely good income. True to his politics, he ruled his Connexion as an enlightened despot, yet, by making workers and traders his travelling preachers and promoting them on merit, he gave a new voice to the aims, grievances and world view of the lower classes.

Wesley's internal world was an intriguing marriage of heart and head. In many ways he was a classic product of the Enlightenment, besotted with the power of reason. He had a confidence in (his own) logic and observation as windows on to absolute truth that left no room for open-mindedness, self-doubt or intellectual toleration. His extraordinary claim to the Scottish minister Ralph Erskine, 'Difference of opinion is indeed with me a very small thing,' was possible only because he considered most of his opinions to be matters of fact. His propensity to insist, amid fiery dispute, that his side of the story was 'plain demonstrable fact' was exasperating. Yet Wesley did more than anyone to reintroduce the religion of the heart into 18th-century England. Methodism was full of music and excitement, dreams and divine impulses, emotional turmoil and mass fervour. What was called fanaticism, Wesley insisted, 'is no more than heart-religion; in other words, "righteousness, and peace, and joy in the Holy Ghost". These must be *felt*, or they have no being.' Excluding these from religion leaves it 'a dry, dead carcass'.

He combined a Catholic devotion to the sacraments of the Church with a Pentecostal welcoming of healings, ecstasies and Low Church spontaneity. He had an evangelical horror of trying to satisfy God by good works, but an even greater horror of trying to satisfy God without good works. He was a founding father of evangelicalism, but for his last 20 years, he consistently retreated from its stark certainties.

He prized plain speaking – always willing to point out others' errors and personal faults with utter candour – and appreciated the favour being returned (though more so on the former count than the latter), yet there is a profound lack of candour in his storytelling. His accounts of theological disputes, anti-Methodist conflicts, romantic debacles, religious revivals and his personal profiles all come at the reader with a dizzying degree of spin. To be fair, self-deprecating honesty is a contemporary virtue rather easier than those favoured by Wesley's generation, but still the assumptions that God's doings need, or one's own deserve, to be improved in the telling are surely questionable.

Wesley's appreciation of women's gifts was a small triumph for the spirit of Christ over Christian tradition, but his personal relationships with women were, even according to admirers, an 'inexcusable weakness'. He was surely not – with all due respect to Molly Wesley – an adulterer. It is impossible that he could so perfectly cover his tracks before so many witnesses, who, as the Grace Murray affair shows, were quite willing to turn on a treacherous leader. However, he suffered from a failure to discern between the romantic and pastoral, which blighted his romances and cast a shadow over his pastoring.

Hampson suggested one more Wesleyan paradox: he bore anti-Methodist assaults without the least anger, but challenges from his own preachers enraged him. His words reverberate with the grinding of axe, but there was, indeed, a contrast between Wesley's meekness in the face of the enemy and his imperiousness with his friends.

We see in Wesley's spirituality the disparate influences of High Church Anglicanism, Moravianism and Puritanism, but the very heart of it is a preoccupation all of his own – perfect holiness. This was Wesley's most distinctive contribution to Methodism and the thread that ran through his personal religion throughout his life. Perfect holiness was the goal that consumed him during his Oxford years; the conquest of sin, and not just its forgiveness, was what he most hoped for from his evangelical conversion; a fear of antinomianism is what inspired his great rift with the predestinarians; and the gift of instantaneous perfection was a doctrine for which in later years he was willing to offend the world. Faith, Wesley said, was the door of religion; holiness, 'religion itself'.

The paradoxes and contrasts in Wesley's policies meant that, on his death, the movement was immediately divided by the diverging tendencies that he had held together. The greatest conflict was over whether the Methodists were to be Dissenters or Anglicans. This matter was largely resolved by the 1795 'Plan of Pacification', which allowed any chapel to administer its own sacraments where the majority was in favour. It was, in effect, a final act of separation. Methodism was a church.

Splits occurred as early as 1797, after Alexander Kilham was expelled for advocating democratic politics and attempting to apply those principles to Methodist church government and then founded the Methodist New Connexion. Others left at the same time over the right to meet in workers' cottages without clerical supervision. The Primitive Methodists were founded in 1811, after Hugh Bourne was expelled for his uncouth and outdated idea of preaching in fields.

The Conference's inevitable drift into conservative respectability was accelerated by the transformation of the lay preachers into an ordained clergy and the struggle towards legal emancipation. Yet, as ever, the bulk of membership came from the working classes – partly because the flexibility of Methodist organization made it far more successful than the Church of England at reaching the new industrial towns. This helped to maintain the egalitarian side of Methodism at the grass roots and, to the horror of its leaders, there was significant Methodist involvement in some of the radical political movements of the 19th century.

Methodist numbers continued to soar throughout the century after Wesley's death. He left behind him 72,000 in the British Isles and 60,000 in America, but by 1851, British membership was around 440,000. (This was about 9 per cent of the church-going population, though so unevenly spread that in Cornwall, Methodists made up 65 per cent of the population.) American membership was well over a million. Methodists were by no means unique in this explosive growth. Nonconformists as a whole grew remarkably, at the expense of the Church of England, from 6 per cent of church-goers in Wesley's youth to 45.5 per cent in 1851. However, Wesley must take some credit for this too, because the denominations that grew were precisely those that embraced evangelicalism, while those that rejected it declined.

Some 100 years after Wesley's death, Methodist membership of all colours peaked at 6 million throughout the English-speaking world, whereas today there are 33 million in the world. The strongest concentrations are in the United States and South Africa, with significant proportions in the UK and across sub-Saharan Africa.

Such figures by no means exhaust Wesley's importance. His influence stretches beyond Methodism to two other major religious movements: evangelicalism and Pentecostalism. Wesley did not invent evangelicalism – it was a force in the Church of England quite independent of him – but he was undoubtedly one of the main fathers of the movement and a major inspiration for its spread both in the Church and among Dissenters. Evangelicalism has been a dominant, if not the dominant, force in English-speaking religion over the last two centuries and of incalculable social influence.

Pentecostalism is more distant from Wesley, but its roots can be traced directly to his unique teaching of instantaneous perfection. Though respectable Methodists cooled towards it, it repeatedly resurfaced in evangelical churches throughout the 19th century, giving rise to various new 'holiness' denominations, and was increasingly identified with the baptism of the Holy Spirit. When Holiness Methodists added the gift of tongues as the sign of this blessing, they created Pentecostalism – the fastest-growing form of Christianity ever, which, after its first century, is rapidly heading towards a membership of 150 million.

Such thoughts take us a long way from the Fellow of Lincoln College, shut away in his room, picking obsessively over his daily failings. However, if Wesley's impact on the world has been phenomenal, it is not a mere accident, because he was a phenomenon in his own right. At fairly sober estimates, he rode 250,000 miles, gave away £30,000 (an amount that could have kept a gentleman for a decade), and preached more than 40,000 sermons. He was a man of rare ability, passion and commitment and unique energy.

However, as Toplady was quick to point out, the Devil is also busy. Energy is only as good as the cause on which it is spent. Wesley's religion had its darker side – its puritanical streak placed harsh restrictions on those impoverished workers who most deserved some innocent diversion; its talk of brotherly love was too often betrayed by fratricidal warfare; its willingness (at a peak from which Wesley later descended) to write off all non-evangelicals as 'almost Christians' was narrow-minded; its tendency to excite convulsions does not suggest a well-balanced collective psyche; and its promises of such things as absolute faith and instant perfection raised unrealistic hopes among its followers.

However, it brought new spiritual life to tens of thousands, offering inspiration, hope, comfort and strength; it fed the hungry, clothed the ragged, healed the sick and employed the destitute; it withstood savage assaults with Christlike courage; it gave a voice and self-confidence to ordinary people; it valued women; and it sought out an abandoned and dangerous underclass with the life-changing message of their acceptance by and value to God. It was balm in a cruel century. 'This love of God and all mankind we believe to be the medicine of life,' Wesley said and the story of his life bears him out. 'Wherever this is, there are virtue and happiness going hand in hand.'

Bibliography of works cited in this book

Ayling, Stanley, *John Wesley*, Collins, 1979.

Baker, Frank (ed.), *The Works of John Wesley*, XXV and XXVI: Letters I (1721–39) and II (1749–55), Clarendon Press, 1980, 1982.

Churnock, Nehemiah (ed.), *The Journal of John Wesley* (8 vols), Charles H. Kelly, 1909–16.

Green, V.H.H., *The Young Mr Wesley*, St Martin's Press, 1961.

Green, V.H.H., *John Wesley*, Nelson, 1964.

Hampson, John, *Memoirs of John Wesley*, 1791.

Hylson-Smith, Kenneth, *The Churches in England from Elizabeth I to Elizabeth II*, SCM Press, 1997.

Jackson, T., *Lives of the Early Methodist Preachers*, 1872.

Jackson, Thomas (ed.), *The Journal of Charles Wesley* (2 vols), Beacon Hill Press, 1909.

Jackson, Thomas (ed.), *The Works of the Rev. John Wesley, A.M.* (14 vols), Wesleyan-Methodist Book Room, 1872.

Léger, J. Augustin, *John Wesley's Last Love*, J.M. Dent & Sons, 1910.

Lloyd, Gareth, '"Running After Strange Women": An insight into John Wesley's troubled marriage from a newly discovered manuscript written by his wife', *Proceedings of the Wesley Historical Society*, LIII, part 5, p. 173.

The Methodist Hymn-Book, Methodist Conference Office, 1933.

Moore, Henry, *The Life of the Rev. John Wesley*, 1824.

Murray, Iain (ed.), *George Whitefield's Journals*, Banner of Truth, 1960.

Outler, Albert C. (ed.), *The Works of John Wesley*, I–IV: Sermons, Abingdon Press, 1984–87.

Rack, Henry, *Reasonable Enthusiast: John Wesley and the Rise of Methodism* (third edition), Epworth Press, 2002.

Telford, John (ed.), *The Letters of John Wesley* (8 vols), Epworth Press, 1931.

Tyerman, Luke, *Life and Times of John Wesley*, 1871.

NOTES

Abbreviations:

JWJ: *The Journal of John Wesley* (8 vols), ed. Nehemiah Churnock, Charles H. Kelly, 1909–16.

JWL: *The Letters of John Wesley* (8 vols), ed. John Telford, Epworth Press, 1931.

JWL (B): *The Works of John Wesley*, XXV and XXVI: Letters I (1721–39) and II (1749–55), ed. Frank Baker, Clarendon Press, 1980, 1982.

JWS: *The Works of John Wesley*, I–IV: *Sermons*, ed. Albert C. Outler, Abingdon Press, 1984–87.

JWW: *The Works of the Rev. John Wesley, A.M.* (14 vols), ed. Thomas Jackson, Wesleyan-Methodist Book Room, 1872.

CWJ: *The Journal of Charles Wesley* (2 vols), ed. Thomas Jackson, Beacon Hill Press, 1909.

p. 7: '... than ever I have been' – manuscript at Wesley College Bristol. Copy in the Museum of Methodism at Wesley's Chapel Leysian Centre, London.

p. 11: '... to live happily together' – V.H.H. Green, *The Young Mr Wesley*, St Martin's Press, 1961, pp. 49–50; Henry Rack, *Reasonable Enthusiast: John Wesley and the Rise of Methodism*, 3rd edn, Epworth Press, 2002, pp. 48–49.

p. 14: '... learned to read well' – JWL (B), I, 24/7/1732; JWJ, 1/8/1742.

p. 15: '... reformed without some difficulty' – Green, *The Young Mr Wesley*, p. 54.

p. 18: '... as fast as he can' – Rack, *Reasonable Enthusiast*, p. 59.

p. 18: '... given me in baptism' – JWJ, 24/5/1738.

p. 18: '... since I was 12 years old' – Rack, *Reasonable Enthusiast*, p. 59.

p. 19: '... Let me hear no more' – Green, *The Young Mr Wesley*, pp. 57–58.

p. 22: '... but a poor purchase' – JWL (B), I, 1/11/1724.

p. 23: '... reasonable hope of salvation' – JWL (B), I, 23/2/1724.

p. 26: '... to imitate his example' – JWJ, I, p. 48.

p. 26: '... my holiness or usefulness' – JWL (B), I, 19/2/1755.

p. 27: '... I modelled my life' – JWJ, 24/5/1738.

p. 28: '... and fear the consequences' – Green, *The Young Mr Wesley*, pp. 208–209; JWL (B), I, 29/11/1726.

p. 28: '... a woman's breasts again' – Rack, *Reasonable Enthusiast*, p. 79.

p. 36: '... too great for your body' – JWL (B), I, 17/11/1731, 11/12/1731, 1/1/1732.

p. 38: '... no longer the whole story' – 'The Circumcision of the Heart', in JWS, I, p. 1.

p. 38: '... I can do nothing' – JWL (B), I, 17/8/1733.

p. 39: '... wanted to change tutor' – JWL (B), I, 14/1/1734.

p. 40: '... compassion for others' – JWL (B), I, 15/1/1734, 31/1/1734, 15/3/1734.

p. 40: '... promote holiness in others' – JWL (B), I, 15/11/1734.

p. 41: '... "trifling acquaintance" and "impertinent company"' – JWL (B), I, 20/11/1734, 10/12/1734 (section 23);

Stanley Ayling, *John Wesley*, Collins, 1979, p. 59.

p. 45: '... on his spiritual journey' – JWJ, 30/1/1736, 23/11/1735, 23/1/1736.

p. 45: '... are not afraid to die' – JWJ, 25/1/1736.

p. 48: '... they were vain words' – JWJ, 7/2/1736.

p. 48: '... Peter the fisherman, presided' – JWJ, 28/2/1736.

p. 51: '... nobody will come to hear you' – JWJ, 22/6/1736.

p. 51: '... none of them after the flesh' – JWL (B), I, 22/3/1736.

p. 58: '... you will preach faith' – JWJ, 5/3/1738.

p. 59: '... talkativeness and vanity' – JWJ, 16/3/1738, 21/3/1738.

p. 59: '... you was a great hypocrite' – Rack, *Reasonable Enthusiast*, p. 184.

p. 60: '... last time of meeting' – JWJ, 1/5/1738.

p. 60: '... kept me from falling' – CWJ, 21/5/1738.

p. 61: '... law of sin and death' – JWJ, 24/5/1738.

p. 62: '... I was always conqueror' – JWJ, 27/5/1738.

p. 62: '... dissimulation in many cases?' – JWL, 7/7/1738, 27/9/1738–28/9/1738.

p. 65: '... these were his "living arguments"' – JWJ, 5/11/1738; JWL (B), I, 4/4/1739.

p. 66: '... acknowledge Thee to be the Lord' – JWJ, 5/1/1739, 6/3/1739, 1/1/1739.

p. 67: '... I am not a Christian' – JWJ, 4/1/1739.

p. 67: '... hosannas of the multitude' – Iain Murray (ed.), *George Whitefield's Journals*, Banner of Truth, 1960, pp. 88–89.

p. 68: '... now broken the ice!' – Murray (ed.), *George Whitefield's Journals*, 28/8/1738, 17/2/1739.

p. 69: '... year of the Lord (Luke 4:18–19)' – JWJ, 2/4/1739.

p. 70: '... master of others' emotions' – John Hampson, *Memoirs of John Wesley* (3 vols), III, 1791, pp. 172–73.

p. 70: '... evidence for what he said' – T. Jackson, *Lives of the Early Methodist Preachers* (6 vols), I, 1872, p. 16; Kenneth Hylson-Smith, *The Churches in England from Elizabeth I to Elizabeth II* (3 vols), II, p. 86; Hampson, *Memoirs of John Wesley*, III, pp. 166–69.

p. 71: '... were accepted by God' – JWJ, 17/4/1739.

p. 72: '... promise of the Father' – JWL (B), I, 30/5/1739; JWJ, 26/4/1739.

p. 72: '... and brought her relief' – JWJ, 30/4/1739, 1/5/1739, 2/5/1739.

p. 73: '... the soul of sin' – JWL (B), I, 10/5/1739; II, 22/8/1744.

p. 77: '... only to look at me' – JWJ, 7/5/1739, 5/6/1739.

p. 77: '... "perish for lack of knowledge"' – JWJ, 11/6/1739; JWL (B), I, 28/5/1739, 22/7/1739.

p. 79: '... violent agony as the rest' – JWJ, 15/6/1739.

p. 83: '... unto God their Saviour' – JWJ, 27/11/1739.

p. 87: '... power to sow the seed' – JWL (B), II, 25/1/1740.

p. 88: '... stillness beliefs frustratingly unreliable' – JWL (B), II, 8/9/1746.

p. 89: '... gave them up to God' – JWJ, 19/12/1740, 23/4/1740, 15/7/1740.

p. 90: '... was willing to remember' – JWJ, 9/5/1740.

p. 90: '... and dispersed the crowd' – JWJ, 1/4/1740.

p. 91: '... dismissed me with many blessings' – JWJ, 14/9/1740.

p. 93: '... opposition on other issues' – JWL (B), 25/4/1741.

p. 94: '... wheresoever he preached at all' – JWL (B), 1/2/1741, 28/3/1741.

p. 97: '... good-natured gentleman' – JWJ, 8/6/1741.

p. 98: '... since my landing in America' – JWJ, 17/4/1741.

p. 100: '... any noise or interruption' – JWJ, 19/3/1742.

p. 103: '... Wesley's palette very nicely' – JWJ, 20/5/1742.

p. 104: '... to resume his rounds' – JWJ, 2/6/1742–12/6/1742.

p. 104: '... as I should have done' – JWJ, 1/8/1742; JWL (B), II, 31/7/1742.

p. 105: '... carefulness and without distraction' – JWL (B), II, 17/11/1742.

p. 105: '... pray for a lowly heart' – JWJ, 2/12/1742.

p. 106: '... philosophically account for it' – JWJ, 25/12/1742.

p. 106: '... with the peace of God' – JWJ, 27/12/1742.

p. 112: '... could not kill one man' – JWJ, 20/10/1743; CWJ, 25/10/1743.

p. 113: '... people came again to see it?' – JWJ, 2/11/1743.

p. 114: '... "I wish you was in hell"' – JWJ, 4/7/1745.

p. 116: '... a thief and a robber' – 'An Earnest Appeal to Men of Reason and Religion', JWW, VIII, section 94, p. 96.

p. 120: '... to guide us to Oakhill' – JWJ, 12/2/1748.

p. 122: '... went to a third edition' – J. Augustin Léger, *John Wesley's Last Love*, J.M. Dent & Sons, 1910, p. 1; JWL, II, 25/6/1746 (section 5), 25/4/1749.

p. 122: '... drops before a shower' – JWJ, 14/4/1748; JWL (B), II, 16/4/1748.

p. 124: '... shall part no more' – JWL (B), II, 7/9/1749.

p. 126: '... happiest person among us' – CWJ, 8/4/1749.

p. 126: '... give us thankful hearts' – JWJ, 16/5/1749.

p. 127: '... His passion revived' – Léger, *John Wesley's Last Love*, p. 6.

p. 129: '... blind and impetuous passion!' – JWL (B), II, 7/9/1749.

p. 131: '... or behaves indecently' – JWL (B), II, 2/10/1749.

p. 132: '... at Dublin she had said, "I do"' – JWL (B), II, 25/9/1749.

p. 133: '... my Will more resigned' – Léger, *John Wesley's Last Love*, p. 86.

p. 136: '... not in their bargain' – JWJ, 31/5/1750.

p. 138: '... suffered so much for us?' – JWL (B), II, 11/3/1751.

p. 139: '"... vain janglings" was heartbreaking' – CWJ, 6/7/1751.

p. 140: '... following throughout his life' – JWJ, 8/7/1751; CWJ, 11/6/1751–28/6/1751.

p. 143: '... *moment* return no more!' – JWL (B), II, 22/5/1752.

p. 143: '... partaking in his hilarity' – Hampson, *Memoirs of John Wesley*, III, p. 178.

p. 144: '... she had finally recovered' – JWL, 5/6/1752.

p. 145: '... Christ's everlasting arms' – JWL (B), 3/12/1753.

p. 147: '... as broke from chains' – JWL (B), 29/4/1755, 31/8/1755.

p. 150: '... in haste for that' – JWL (B), II, 20/6/1755.

p. 151: '... it is all over. Adieu' – JWL (B), II, 24/9/1755.

p. 152: '... able to bear its weight' – JWL (B), II, 5/9/1755,

p. 154: '... straight into his presence' – JWL, 8/11/1757–20/1/1758.

p. 154: '... words I could devise' – JWL, 10/2/1758.

p. 155: '... and my own conscience' – JWL, 12/7/1758.

p. 157: '... the blood of Christ!' – JWJ, 30/5/1759.

p. 157: '… God takes you to himself' – JWL, 5/4/1758.

p. 158: '… walk in the light continually' – JWJ, 6/3/1760.

p. 159: '… Bid me do *anything, everything*' – JWL, 9/4/1759, 23/3/1760.

p. 159: '… character is at stake' – Gareth Lloyd, '"Running After Strange Women": An insight into John Wesley's troubled marriage from a newly discovered manuscript written by his wife', *Proceedings of the Wesley Historical Society*, LIII, part 5, p. 173.

p. 160: '… Go on calmly and steadily' – JWL, 14/2/1761.

p. 161: '… rejoicing with joy unspeakable' – JWJ, 23/6/1761, 4/3/1761.

p. 161: '… one that beateth the air?' – JWJ, 21/5/1761.

p. 161: '… day of their visitation' – JWJ, 21/9/1761.

p. 163: '… asleep by 10 o'clock' – JWJ, 28/2/1763.

p. 164: '… they have now lost both' – 'A Plain Account of Christian Perfection', JWW, XI, section 25, Q.30.

p. 167: '… God had called him' – Henry Moore, *The Life of the Rev. John Wesley* (2 vols), II, 1824, p. 175.

p. 168: '… entangled therein and perish?' – JWJ, 18/9/1763.

p. 168: '… come to what I do not know' – JWL, 27/6/1766.

p. 169: '… the results if he had' – Rack, *Reasonable Enthusiast*, p. 486.

p. 170: '… Witness my hand, A– T–' – 'The Doctrine of Absolute Predestination Stated and Asserted by the Rev'd A– T–', JWW, XIV.

p. 171: '… concluded Wesley, "about words"' – 'Minutes of Some Late Conversations', JWW, VIII.

p. 172: '… may "agree to disagree"' – 'On the Death of Mr Whitefield', JWS, II (III.1).

p. 178: '… was ready to strike' – JWL, 14/6/1775.

p. 179: '… record of their meeting' – Luke Tyerman, *The Life and Times of John Wesley* (3 vols), II, 1871, p. 113; JWL, 15/7/1774.

p. 180: '… doing these thirty years?' – JWL, 15/12/1772.

p. 180: '… never speak to him again' – JWL, 28/4/1775.

p. 181: '… soon be worn threadbare' – Wesley's introduction in *The Methodist Hymn-Book*, Methodist Conference Office, 1933.

p. 183: '… over his whole person' – Hampson, *Memoirs of John Wesley*, III, p. 168.

p. 188: '… see my face no more' – JWJ, 24/10/1786, 2/1/1787.

p. 189: '… tied Methodism to the Church' – JWL, 20/9/1788.

p. 189: '… put a full end to this!' – JWL, 20/9/1788.

p. 192: '… life stand still at last' – JWJ, 1/1/90, 28/6/1790.

p. 193: '… Your affectionate servant, / John Wesley' – JWL, 24/2/1791.

p. 196: '… a dry, dead carcass' – JWJ, 15/8/1771.

p. 197: '… an "inexcusable weakness"' – John Pawson, quoted in Lloyd, 'Running After Strange Women', p. 174.

INDEX